NASCAR

THE DEFINITIVE HISTORY OF
AMERICA'S SPORT

Daytona Beach-Road course

The shifting sands of Daytona Beach provided a landscape for early NASCAR racing. In 1950, NASCAR Modifieds raced into the north turn on the Daytona Beach-Road course, headed for the asphalt stretch of Highway A1A.

//// NASCAR

THE DEFINITIVE HISTORY OF
AMERICA'S SPORT

MIKE HEMBREE

FOREWORD BY JOE GIBBS

HarperEntertainment
An Imprint of HarperCollins*Publishers*

A TEHABI BOOK

ACKNOWLEDGMENTS

*The author wishes to acknowledge the influence of Leslie Timms Jr., boss, mentor, and friend, who created a mold
for what sportswriters should be. A tip of the victory lane cap to the work of stock car racing historians Greg Fielden, Gene
Granger, and Bob Latford, whose digging in imposing stacks of old records, result sheets, record books, and newspaper files
has documented much of the sport's foundation. Special thanks, too, to Jim Hunter, Bob Moore,
Kevin Triplett, Tim Sullivan, Buz McKim, and the legions of team and company representatives who have worked
in the sport over the years. And a salute to the memory of two great auto racing journalists, Joe Whitlock and
George Cunningham, who wrote about the sport with fire and eloquence.*

TEHABI BOOKS

NASCAR: *The Definitive History of America's Sport* was conceived
and produced by Tehabi Books. Tehabi—symbolizing the spirit of
teamwork—derives its name from the Hopi Indian tribe of the
southwestern United States. As an award-winning book producer,
Tehabi works with national and international publishers, corporations,
institutions, and nonprofit groups to identify, develop, and implement
comprehensive publishing programs. Tehabi Books is located in
Del Mar, California. www.tehabi.com

Chris Capen, *President*
Tom Lewis, *Editorial and Design Director*
Sharon Lewis, *Controller*
Nancy Cash, *Managing Editor*
Andy Lewis, *Senior Art Director*
Sarah Morgans, *Associate Editor*
Maria Medina, *Administrative Assistant*
Curtis Boyer, *Production Artist*
Mo Latimer, *Materials Manager*
Sam Lewis, *Webmaster*
Kristin Connelly, *Systems Administrator*
Tim Connolly, *Sales and Marketing Manager*
Tiffany Smith, *Executive Assistant*
Gail Fink, *Copy Editor*
Kathi George, *Proofreader*
Ken DellaPenta, *Indexer*

Photography credits appear on page 203.

This edition is printed on acid-free paper that meets the American
National Standards Institute Z39.48 standard.
Printed in Hong Kong through Dai Nippon Printing Co., Ltd.

HarperEntertainment

An Imprint of HarperCollinsPublishers

NASCAR: *The Definitive History of America's Sport* is published by
HarperEntertainment, an Imprint of HarperCollins Publishers Inc.,
10 East 53rd Street, New York, NY 10022. www.harpercollins.com
    Tom Dupree, *Executive Editor*
    Frank Fochetta, *Vice President and Director of HarperCollins Enterprises*
    Helen Moore, *Publishing Manager*
    Susan Sanguily, *Creative Director*
    April Benavides, *Production Editor*

With special thanks to key individuals at NASCAR for their
contributions in the creation of NASCAR: *The Definitive History of
America's Sport:*
    Kelly Crouch, *Director of Special Projects and Publishing*
    Jennifer White, *Editorial Manager*
    Paul Schaefer, *Senior Editor*
    Buz McKim, *NASCAR Archivist*
With thanks to Dorothy Beech, Judy Jones, Bob Mauk, and Ann Nicely.

NASCAR is a registered trademark of the National Association for Stock
Car Auto Racing, Inc. www.nascar.com

Library of Congress Cataloging-in-Publication Data is available.
ISBN 0-06-105080-6

00 01 02 03 04 / TB 10 9 8 7 6 5 4 3 2 1

Fans have always invented creative contraptions to attain a better infield vantage point. Here fans observe the Speedweeks in Daytona festivities.

Table of Contents

Flags over Texas

The symbol of racing victory waves in the morning breeze before the 1998 Texas 500 at Texas Motor Speedway. The 500 is one of thirty-four NASCAR Winston Cup Series races each season.

The scene at the start of a NASCAR race has changed dramatically since the early days on the Daytona Beach-Road course. Fine-tuned modern racers line up behind the pace car to begin a race, leaving their uniformed crews behind the pit-road wall to prepare for a day's work. At a beach race, mechanics and other associates of drivers would mill about on the track in the minutes before the event began.

The duel

Fender-to-fender, door-to-door competition has been a NASCAR theme for more than a half-century. Joe Weatherly (No. 12) and Johnny Allen battle at Daytona International Speedway in the Firecracker 250 in 1959, while current-day racers Mike Skinner (No. 31), Rusty Wallace (No. 2), and Jeff Gordon (No. 24) run three-abreast at top speeds.

Close quarters

NASCAR action has always been fast, furious, and incredibly close. From the days of the Daytona Beach-Road course, where Fireball Roberts (No. 22) fights a tight battle for position in the turn, to modern short tracks, where bumper-to-bumper racing is par for the course, NASCAR drivers have created some of motorsports' most exhilarating competition.

Frantic finishes

Jeff Burton (No. 99) leads a pack of traffic toward
the checkered flag in the 1999 Coca-Cola 600 at
Lowe's Motor Speedway. Richard Petty shadows
David Pearson as they run toward the finish in
the 1972 Firecracker 500.

A win used to be the triumph of a single man, with a little help from his friends, in the day of five-time NASCAR short-track champion and 1959 Southern 500 winner Jim Reed. But today, even when a driver owns his car, as did 1997 Brickyard 400 winner Ricky Rudd, he owes much of his success to his crew.

When I take a step back and look at all that's happened to me in my life so far, I consider myself blessed to have had the chance to be involved in the Great American Sport. I'm not talking about football or baseball. I'm talking about the incredibly rewarding time I've spent involved with NASCAR.

Some people might be a little struck by my naming NASCAR racing as the Great American Sport. But let's look at this: The values we hold true as Americans—hard work, faith, family, and community—have all been abundant in NASCAR during its fifty-plus-year history. NASCAR was born out of the vision of one man, Bill France Sr., and the backing of dozens of daring drivers. Across

five decades this sport has thrived from the sweat, hope, and close ties of those first men—and women—who raced their family sedans around dusty bullrings on warm summer evenings. It's that history that drew me to the sport and that history that the following pages honor.

When you look at the speed, efficiency, and teamwork of a NASCAR pit crew, you can't help but marvel at the hours of intensive practice that go into making each teammate's choreographed move interact precisely with that of his fellow teammates. As a three-time Super Bowl–winning coach, I've seen first-hand the hard work and dedication it takes to have a successful football team. That same level of intensity is evident in

THE
GREAT AMERICAN SPORT
BY JOE GIBBS

those pit crew members who put everything they have into their jobs, knowing that the success of the entire team rests with each of them. The same goes for NASCAR drivers. From Fireball Roberts to Dale Earnhardt, their skill and concentration come from years of dedication to preparing themselves for the limelight of NASCAR. The hard work and long hours they have endured are a testament to their grit and determination.

From the Frances to the Pettys to the Flocks to the Bodines to the Earnhardts to the Jarretts, NASCAR has always been a community made up largely of families sharing time and effort together. Family is such a common theme in NASCAR—and a lasting legacy from the sport's first years on the rutted dirt tracks of the South. I see my own participation in the sport as a family affair. My sons J. D. and Coy both have begun careers as drivers, which is so

From the Frances to the Pettys to the Flocks to the Bodines to the Earnhardts to the Jarretts, NASCAR has always been a community made up largely of families sharing time and effort together.

exciting for me and my family, and I can not fully explain how blessed I feel to have both my sons working with me at Joe Gibbs Racing. My wife Pat enjoys race days as much as I do, and my young grandchildren will soon be coming out to the track.

But my family's experience with NASCAR is certainly not unique. I'm always most aware of that when I look across the infield or up into the stands at the legions of fans that turn out each weekend to root for their team and their sport. Take one look at the license plates in the parking lot and you'll know that fans travel great distances to share in the experience of NASCAR racing.

So you can see why my impressions of this sport are so glowing. From one man's dreams, NASCAR has grown to what it is today: a national pastime. NASCAR racing is indeed an all-American sport that has risen to the level of greatness.

Jim Paschal rolled into town from nearby High Point with his father's 1946 Ford—and his father's blessing. No small thing on this day, for the afternoon would be filled with noise and fury, with the summertime thunder of stock car racing, with the chill of high adventure.

Herb Thomas, a young man fresh off the farm, showed up in a Ford. Little Bill Blair was in a hot-rod Lincoln, Bob Flock would wrestle a monster Hudson, and Jim Roper was set to drive the No. 34 Lincoln after crossing half the continent to get the chance.

Watching from the stands was an eleven-year-old kid named Richard Lee Petty. He had a father in the race, a grin as wide as Nebraska, and a future beyond his wildest dreams.

And there were others. More than thirteen thousand others, by most counts.

It was June 19, 1949. Charlotte Speedway, a rut-filled, three-quarter-mile dirt speedway, was the temporary center of the universe for thirty-three drivers and their hulking automobiles, almost all showroom black with crudely painted numbers on their doors. As they circled the track before the drop of the green flag by starter Alvin Hawkins, their engines heralded the birth of the National Association for Stock Car Auto Racing's Strictly Stock Series, now known worldwide as NASCAR Winston Cup Series racing.

BIG BILL,
BIG DREAMS

Formed from clay

Dirt tracks, many carved from the red clay of the Southeast, were the first battlegrounds for the souped-up jalopies, opposite, of the early Modified years. Bill France Sr., left, raced these vehicles in the 1940s.

NASCAR, as it would be called virtually from its first day, had been formed eighteen months earlier and had sanctioned dozens of other races, but on this day in Charlotte, North Carolina, on a track carved from Piedmont clay, the anchor was fixed in place. The world's newest major auto racing sanctioning body was displaying its new product—a class for pure stock cars with virtually no modifications (thus, Strictly Stock). It was founder Bill France's idea. The public would respond with enthusiasm to racing that involved cars almost identical to the ones driven on the highway, he reasoned. And he was right.

More than a half-century later, NASCAR Winston Cup stars Jeff Gordon, Dale Jarrett, Mark Martin, and Dale Earnhardt race on a foundation built on the settled dust of that June afternoon in North Carolina. Their purpose-built race cars are a world removed from the big beasts that pounded Charlotte Speedway in Strictly Stock Race No. 1, but the heart of stock car racing beats much as it did then—with the daredevil spirit of men and women willing to drive to the ragged edge and, occasionally, beyond.

How thirty-three race car drivers came to assemble at Charlotte Speedway to begin a new era of auto racing is a story that begins the day the second automobile was assembled. It's a tale that runs through moonlit nights in the high mountains of the Carolinas and Georgia, through hot and fast afternoons on the sand of Daytona Beach, and through the life and times of William Henry Getty France, the man at its center.

> It has been said that the only prerequisite for auto racing was the construction of two cars. The concept is as simple as it is intriguing: My car can beat your car.

It has been said that the only prerequisite for auto racing was the construction of two cars. Of course, there is no evidence that the first two cars ever built were matched in any sort of contest, but the concept is as simple as it is intriguing: My car can beat your car.

Before the arrival of the twentieth century, various "races" were held across the country as prominent individuals and companies intrigued with this new mode of travel sponsored events that required competitors to drive their new horseless carriages from one point to another, typically from city to city. In 1896, the Rhode Island State Fair Association hosted several days of short automobile races on the one-mile Narragansett Park horse track, ushering in the era of oval-track racing in the United States.

On the hard-packed sands of Florida's east coast, the idea of racing automobiles became reality in 1903. At Ormond Beach, north of Daytona, wealthy winter visitors to the resort area eyed the long, flat beach stretches as an ideal landscape for tinkering with their toys. Ransom Olds, of Oldsmobile fame, and Alexander Winton, who began building cars in 1896, tested the strength of their cars in timed runs on the beach. Their competition began several decades of "land speed record runs" at Ormond and Daytona, attracting such luminaries as Henry Ford, Louis Chevrolet, William Vanderbilt, and Barney Oldfield, who, in 1904, was clocked at almost 84 miles per hour on the beach in a Winton powered by a pair of four-cylinder engines.

Pioneers

Racing on the Daytona Beach shore in the late 1930s attracted a rich variety of drivers. Opposite: Among the competitors in a 1936 race were (left to right) Indianapolis 500 winner A. T. G. Gardner, "Wild" Bill Cummings, and national dirt-track champion "Doc" MacKinzie. Ormond Beach, north of Daytona, became a headquarters for adventurous drivers in the early years of the twentieth century. Competition between wealthy "gentlemen" drivers of the day matched men like R. E. Olds, top, in the Olds "Pirate," against Alexander Winton in the "Winton Bullet." Barney Oldfield, bottom, in the Winton Bullet No. 2, set world speed records on the beach.

Dirt and sand

Raymond Parks, left, an Atlanta businessman who owned some of the finest race cars of NASCAR's early years, also provided a Cadillac to serve as the pace car on the Daytona Beach-Road course. Above: Now-defunct Lakewood Speedway in Atlanta remains a fabled track where Fonty Flock, opposite, swapped his car for his brother Tim's ailing Hudson Hornet on the track in turn four.

At Indianapolis and elsewhere in the Midwest, daring drivers were putting some of the first true oval-track race cars to power and endurance tests on tracks large and small. The American Automobile Association (AAA) began sanctioning races in 1904.

In the South of the pre–World War II era, good ol' boys from the moonshine whiskey culture of the southern Appalachian Mountains and shade-tree mechanics who tinkered with old family coupes were challenging each other on the first generation of racetracks. Some were little more than dirt circles cut from cow pastures. Others, like the wicked one-mile Lakewood Speedway in Atlanta, were substantial speedways for their time. Atlanta, in fact, became an early gathering place of sorts for dozens of Carolina and Georgia drivers who loved the thrill of speed and the opportunity to trade fender licks with others of the daredevil breed.

"There were plenty of good drivers right around there," said Jack Smith, one of the most successful of stock car racing's rough-and-tumble early days. "Red Byron, Gober Sosebee, the Flock brothers. You'd run the Peach Bowl in Atlanta on a Sunday; Vidalia, Georgia, on Monday; back to the Peach Bowl on Wednesday; over into South Carolina on Thursday; and then wherever was paying the most the rest of the week. You could run all those based out of Atlanta. You only had one car, of course. You just straightened out the front

> "You only had one car, of course. You knew you had to finish that race and the one the next night or you weren't going to eat good that week."
> — DRIVER JACK SMITH

axle or maybe put a rear end under it, and went on. You knew you had to finish that race and the one the next night somewhere else or you weren't going to eat good that week."

Businessman Raymond Parks was a key figure in Atlanta racing circles in the 1930s and '40s. With links to the moonshine runners who made lightning trips to and from the north Georgia mountains and other highland delivery points, Parks became fast friends with some of the best racers of the day, hard-driving men like Lloyd Seay and Roy Hall. They sought—and received—backing from Parks, whose various business endeavors provided him with enough money to buy the best cars and, more important, the best mechanic.

His name was Louis "Red" Vogt, and his Atlanta garage churned out hot cars for liquor runners and stock car racers (sometimes, one and the same). Vogt, who in 1916 had started working in a Cadillac garage in Washington, D.C., at the age of twelve, moved to Atlanta in the mid-1920s, opened his own garage, and soon was building racers for sprint, midget, Indy-car, and modified drivers. Called "the grandfather of all stock car racing mechanics" by no less a personage than Smokey Yunick, another of the great wrenches, Vogt built hundreds of race-winning engines in several decades in the sport. Hall, Seay, Bob and Fonty Flock, and Red Byron drove Vogt-powered cars to strings of victories. Vogt's business went well enough to support the purchase of a full-page advertisement in a 1949 issue of *Speed Age* auto racing magazine in which he announced that "Due to the close of the present Stock Car Racing Season, we will have time to build a limited number of racing engines for our customers."

Big Bill, two Reds

Bill France Sr. is flanked by two heavyweights from NASCAR's formative years: superstar mechanic Red Vogt (left) and driver Red Byron, who won the first Strictly Stock championship in 1949. Opposite: Even in the early days, a NASCAR race drew enough fans to fill the stands.

Seay, many old-timers say, could have been one of NASCAR's early stars. He never got the chance. He died September 2, 1941, of a gunshot wound to the stomach after being involved in an argument over a moonshine-related payment. In a cemetery in Dawsonville, the heartland of north Georgia racing, Seay's large headstone includes a carving of a race car with an insert of his photo. The bill for the unique memorial was paid by Raymond Parks.

Along the slopes of the North Carolina mountains, Robert Glenn Johnson Jr.—"Junior" to everyone—was learning the family trade of moonshine-making and "tripping," the fine art of hauling the illegal brew to various points east and south. He also worked on the family farm, and he was standing behind a plow there, barefoot, in the summer of 1949 when his brother L. P. stopped by and offered him the chance to drive in a race. On the spot, he became one of the brethren, those unlikely wild men who would try almost anything, particularly if it held the scent of danger and adventure.

Before his first race, nobody told Johnson what to do. He had been to school on long whiskey-hauling runs in and out of the mountains, pushing souped-up Ford coupes to their limits, staying a turn ahead of the law.

"I felt like I knew what to do," Johnson said matter-of-factly. "I had done my homework on knowing how to drive a car when I ran hauling moonshine. I had to deal with the revenue agents, the sheriff, the ABC officers—all kinds. To be able to outrun them and keep from getting caught, I had to be very skillful, and that's what I did. When I showed up at the racetrack, that's just exactly what I'd been doing for several years. So I did have one up on the competitors."

Racing on the Daytona Beach sand, a wild experience that ultimately would attract Johnson, lured would-be heroes from all over. Joe Littlejohn, living in Spartanburg, South Carolina, heard about the Daytona races in 1938 and impulsively drove south to see what was going on. Told he needed to check with a gentleman named Bill

France at the town Amoco station, Littlejohn drove over, met France, and soon was churning sand along the Daytona shore with the rest of the unlikely band of pioneers.

Inspired by this brush with competitive racing, Littlejohn returned to Spartanburg and, in the fall of 1939, made a deal with city officials to promote auto races at the local Piedmont Interstate Fairgrounds track. It wasn't an easy sell. "I went to talk to city council, and they said, 'What in the world do you want to do, kill everybody in Spartanburg?' I said, 'No, I'm not planning on hurting anybody.' They finally agreed to let me use it."

Some of the best drivers of racing's early years would run at the half-mile oval.

Other short dirt tracks popped up around the Southeast. Typical of them was Greenville-Pickens Speedway, also in upstate South Carolina. Opened as a horse-racing track, Greenville-Pickens hosted its first stock car race July 4, 1946. Perhaps not surprisingly, Bill France was there to direct it. Although there was not yet a NASCAR, France's promotional skills were well respected. Drivers and fans responded. A crowd of several thousand—newspaper reports put the estimate at eight thousand, probably an exaggeration—turned out for a race-day program that also included mule races and a greased pig chase. Ed Samples, part of the Atlanta hot-car crowd, won the race.

Out front, early

Lloyd Seay, above, roared out of the north Georgia mountains to become a force in the early years of stock car racing. Prior to NASCAR's organization, Seay was a frequent winner on dirt tracks. Opposite: Seay powers through the north turn of the Daytona Beach-Road course in 1941. Driver Junior Johnson, left, said racing on NASCAR ovals in the 1950s was relatively easy compared to the hot-rodding he did while evading authorities to transport moonshine whiskey through the North Carolina mountains.

On the home front

While her husband traveled the country making a name for NASCAR, Anne B. France directed operations in the Daytona Beach office. They posed beside Bill's 1939 Mercury after a 1939 race, below. Until the final years of her life, France worked in the ticket office, below opposite, for a time with her granddaughter Lesa. Lesa and Anne are shown years before they became coworkers, above opposite.

If Bill France Sr. built the foundation for and put the roof on the house that became NASCAR, Anne B. France held the ladder.

Annie B., as she was known in the halls of the NASCAR and Daytona International Speedway offices in Daytona Beach, Florida, married Bill France in Washington, D.C., in 1931 with no idea of the adventure they would live over the next half-century. A native of Nathans Creek, North Carolina, Anne Bledsoe was a nurse at a Washington hospital when she met France, who then was a mechanic.

Three years after their marriage, the Frances left Washington for warmer winters and better opportunities, arriving in Daytona Beach to find a nice ocean side village and—to Bill's delight—an active motorsports community. They settled near downtown.

Fifteen years later, France had set in motion the apparatus that would build his idea—automobile racing for American-built sedans that people drove on Main Street—into the country's number one auto racing series. He had the big plans, the broad concepts. Annie B. had the conservative

common sense that kept things on an even keel and helped to make the dream reality.

"She was involved in pretty much every aspect of the business that [required attention to] details," said Lesa France Kennedy, Anne's granddaughter. They shared an office after Kennedy graduated from Duke University and began working at NASCAR and Daytona International Speedway headquarters, then located near the tunnel entrance to the speedway.

"I guess Pops [Bill Sr.] always has been credited with being the visionary," Kennedy said. "The credit to her was that she was able to handle all the analytical aspects of the business."

NASCAR's first "office" was a room in the France home in Daytona Beach. It became Anne France's headquarters, the place where she kept the business—and the dollars—in line while her husband worked at making his vision real. She sold tickets, paid bills, kept ledgers, and generally made sure things ran smoothly.

It was a job she worked—happily—until the final years of her life.

"She was pretty much keeping an eye on everything the years she worked with me," Kennedy said. "She was still in the ticket department. She was very close to that and to the people who worked in that area. Toward the last, she was a little more part time, but she still made it to the office most days. It was her life. She made it clear that was really what she enjoyed doing.

"The people that had worked with her from the very beginning had a lot of respect for her. They had a really good relationship. That was part of her life, as well. A lot of them remained involved in the business, and she liked to touch base with them."

While her husband was big and bold and usually dominated any room he visited, Anne France was successful in avoiding the spotlight most of her life. Even as the NASCAR and International Speedway Corporation entities grew into giants, she preferred to stay in the background, making sure the figures matched and the tickets were sold.

"She was a very private person," Kennedy said. "Although you could get some stories out of her, she was private. She really shied away from the limelight. It didn't faze her at all. Even as the business grew, she didn't see a need to get involved in areas other than what she was interested in."

A statue near the entrance to Daytona International Speedway honors Bill and Anne France, who, together, built one of the world's most successful sports empires.

Racing in a rut

With fans watching from only a few feet away, John Rutherford leads a 1936 race on the Daytona Beach-Road course. Heavy cars plowing through the sandy turns on the course quickly made ruts in the track.

In southern Virginia, Clay Earles wanted a racetrack, too. He saw a race in Salisbury, North Carolina, in 1946, enjoyed the competition, and saw no reason such an enterprise wouldn't work for him. A deal maker of the first order and a jack-of-all-trades, Earles rounded up some partners and built Martinsville Speedway, a raw half-mile oval. The first race—for modified stock cars—was September 7, 1947. The partnership's investment in the track had reached $60,000. Bill France—that man again—was brought in as promoter.

Two of Raymond Parks's drivers, Red Byron and Bob Flock, drove Fords to a one-two finish in the Martinsville inaugural. How many people in the crowd of more than six thousand saw the finish is a matter of some conjecture, for the speedway was cloaked in a perpetual dust cloud throughout the event. Aware that dust could be a problem, Earles had the track surface coated with twenty thousand gallons of oil, calcium chloride, and water, but on race day the speedway became, as Earles would later describe it, "the dustiest place I've ever seen. When the race started, it looked like someone had dropped a nuclear bomb."

Earles paid a purse of two thousand dollars. Tickets were two dollars.

Tracks like Martinsville and Greenville-Pickens—some better, some immeasurably worse—appeared all over the Southeast in the years immediately after World War II. In 1948, new dirt tracks opened in Charlotte, Greensboro, Lexington, North Wilkesboro, Elkin, and Hillsboro in North Carolina. They featured modified racing, and their shows ranged from splendid to sordid. Some had full fields of cars one week and only a handful the next. Fly-by-night promoters showed up with promises of great things but often left track owners and drivers in the lurch.

Into this fertile landscape stepped Bill France. Born in Washington, D.C., September 26, 1909, France, a talented mechanic and an employee at a couple of automobile dealerships, put together his first race car in 1926 and began racing on dirt tracks around Washington.

> ## "It was the dustiest place I've ever seen. When the race started, it looked like someone had dropped a bomb."
> —Track owner Clay Earles

He and Anne Bledsoe, a nurse France met while attending a hospital dance, married in 1931. In 1934, they decided to move to Miami, Florida, in pursuit of a warmer climate and better jobs. Carrying about twenty-five dollars and France's box of tools, they stopped in Daytona Beach, were enthralled with the beauty of the area, and never left. France, at six-foot-five a rather imposing individual, got a job as a mechanic at Daytona Motor Company but quickly saved enough money to buy and operate an Amoco service station on Main Street.

France was on hand as a spectator March 7, 1935, when British adventurer Malcolm Campbell closed out Daytona's thirty-year run as a land-speed capital by roaring down the Measured Mile course on the beach at a speed of more than 276 mph. After that run, those chasing such records left the Florida coast and headed to the more wide open spaces of the Bonneville Salt Flats in Utah, leaving Daytona with a sudden speed vacuum.

France and others stepped in to fill it.

Daytona city officials, eager to keep the racing fire burning and the crowds it attracted coming to the beach, designed what, at first glance, appeared to be an odd replacement. Using 1.5-mile segments of the beach and the parallel Highway A1A along the seashore, they formed a temporary elongated oval racetrack. The two straightaways were joined on the northern and southern ends of the beach. The AAA sanctioned the first race on the course on March 8, 1936. France entered and finished fifth.

Described by his contemporaries as a smart, patient driver, France raced sporadically from the late 1920s until 1950, winning a national championship of sorts in 1940 and, very late in his driving career, enjoying some fine runs in cars owned

Family of daredevils

Oldest of three racing Flock brothers, Bob raced in NASCAR's first season and ended his career in 1956 with four NASCAR Winston Cup Series victories.

by Raymond Parks. ("He had to be good if he drove for me," Parks has said.) France saw his future on the other side of the driver door, however, and his interest in the organizational aspects of the sport grew in those early years in Daytona. Soon he was promoting races on the Daytona Beach-Road course and at small tracks around the Southeast. For the 1938 race on the beach course, France presented a striking prize list for lap leaders: a bottle of rum, a $2.50 credit at an area men's store, a box of cigars, and a case of motor oil.

During the 1946 season, France promoted a handful of stock car races in the Southeast. From that experience, he saw that bigger meant better and that there was a pressing need for an umbrella organization to unify the ragtag world of stock cars into a "national" group with rules, guaranteed purses, and true championships awards. He got an earful of advice in a meeting with Charlotte, North Carolina, newspaper sports editor Wilton Garrison. Attempting to promote a one-hundred-mile race at the Charlotte fair-grounds track as a "national championship" event, France was told by Garrison that he had to have a legitimate national-level orga-nization with standards, rules, and point standings before mainstream newspapers would accept his winning drivers as "national champions." Partly in response to that chal-lenge, France formed the National Champi-onship Stock Car Circuit (NCSCC) that season and ran races under its banner through 1947. His Daytona Beach service station was headquarters, and there was even a series slogan: Where the fastest that run, run the fastest.

With more and more new tracks appearing around the country and France's new group beginning to flex its muscles, France saw

what the next step should be. He called for an NCSCC meeting in December 1947 in Daytona Beach, but his real goal was to push forward with a bigger and better idea: the beginning of an organization that would link leading drivers, car owners, track owners, and promoters with a national scope.

Scott French lives in NASCAR's nursery.

His two-bedroom apartment is in the penthouse atop the Streamline Hotel, a large pink building at 140 South Atlantic Avenue in Daytona Beach. French is the general manager of the hotel, which, by outside appearances, is no more significant than any of the other older buildings along Daytona's beachside highway.

French's apartment has undergone considerable renovation since the 1940s, however. At that time it was the Ebony Room, a

bar with a porch that provided a high-level view of the Atlantic. The bar fixtures were removed so that the rooftop space could be converted into an apartment.

The Ebony gave birth to NASCAR. Within its walls were held the meetings that resulted in the sanctioning body's formation.

France's invitation list for the Decem-ber 14–17 meetings included promoters Bill Tuthill and Joe Littlejohn; mechanic Red Vogt; and drivers Marshall Teague, Buddy Shuman, and Red Byron, among others. They were to decide, in France's words, "the outcome of stock car racing in the country today."

To Sir with speed

Sir Malcolm Campbell, above, shows wear on tires after his famous Bluebird racer, below, burned the Daytona beach sand on a record run in 1935. Campbell hit 276.82 mph in the Bluebird V.

A break at the beach

On the deck outside the Ebony Room, attendees pose for a photo during the December 1947 meetings that reorganized stock car racing. Kneeling are (left to right) Chick DiNatale, Jimmy Quisenberry, Ed Bruce, Jack Peters, and Alvin Hawkins. Standing are Freddie Horton, Sam Packard, Ed Samples (hidden), Joe Ross, Marshall Teague, Bill Tuthill, Joe Littlejohn, Bob Osiecki, Buddy Shuman, Lucky Sauer (hidden), Tom Galan, Eddie Bland, Bill France Sr., Bob Richards, Harvey Tattersall Jr., Fred Dagaver, Bill Streeter, and Jimmy Cox.

The smoke-filled room

Bill France Sr. (at far end of table) called the meetings
of drivers, officials, and promoters that ended with the
organization of NASCAR. Sitting to France's right is Bill
Tuthill, who moderated the meetings. The top floor of the
Streamline Hotel, opposite, near the Daytona oceanfront
was the setting for the meetings.

On the beach

Adorned in the unusual racing helmets of the day, drivers (left to right) Smokey Purser, Bill France Sr., Roy Hall, and Sam Packard await a run on the beach course. All raced on the beach in the pre–World War II era. Purser once won a beach race and didn't stop for inspection, driving away from the course. He was disqualified.

Reports of attendance numbers at the meetings vary, although it is likely that at least twenty-two and as many as thirty-five men attended one or more sessions. Others probably dropped in and out during the four days, for the Streamline was a regular gathering place for people involved in racing on the nearby beach.

Tuthill moderated the meetings, but the agenda clearly belonged to France. Tuthill, Vogt, Littlejohn, and Teague were among the most vocal of the crowd. On the first day, France opened the proceedings with a speech that lasted most of an hour. "We are all interested in one thing," he said. "That is improving present conditions. The answer lies in our group here today to do it." Among his specific goals, he said, was the elimination of "after-the-race arguments."

There apparently was little serious debate, a remarkable achievement, said participant Sam Packard, because the meetings brought together a mix of "Yankees, Southerners, and bootleggers.

"We all more or less knew each other," said Packard, a racer from Providence, Rhode Island, who moved to Daytona Beach to drive on the Beach-Road course and wound up as an employee at France's service station. "We had been running tracks together. We were all after the same thing."

Benny Kahn, then a sportswriter for the Daytona Beach *News-Journal*, attended the meetings and described the participants as "the owner of a small local filling station; a local race driver; a Providence, Rhode Island, motorcycle dealer; an Atlanta garage operator; a Spartanburg turnip farmer; a New Rochelle, New York, midget racetrack promoter; a moonshiner or two with anonymous addresses; and assorted hustlers."

Joe Epton, an early France confidant who missed the organizational meetings because

of illness, said the lack of assured purses was the primary reason for forming a new, more cohesive stock car racing sanctioning body. "You wanted a guaranteed purse," said Epton, who worked with France as NASCAR's Director of Timing and Scoring for more than forty years. "Before that, some guys would run a race and not take in too much money, and they'd just put the money in a sack and take off. The drivers didn't get anything. We started putting the prize money in envelopes. The drivers would walk up and sign for it and get their money right there after the race." That method would later change as purses increased and distributing large sums of cash at race sites became practically impossible. In the early years, though, the concept was a big plus for NASCAR in its attempts to attract fields of quality cars and drivers.

"We thought the whole thing should have some teeth in it," said Joe Littlejohn in a 1975 interview. "People were racing, and they had to have some rules and regulations and someone to enforce them."

Before the formal meetings, France, Tuthill, and Vogt met and designed a set of proposed rules. Tables in the bar were pushed together to form a conference-type setting, and, with Tuthill serving as moderator, the men talked things over. Photographs of the meeting show pencils, pads, and cigarette packs spread across the tables while cigarette smoke swirls overhead.

The meetings were quite lengthy, Packard explained, because, among other reasons, they took place in a cocktail lounge.

On the final day, after France had been named president of the group and E. G. "Cannonball" Baker, an endurance racer, was elected its first commissioner, participants began discussions on the new organization's name. Two possibilities were

> "Before NASCAR some guys would run a race and not take in too much money, and they'd just put the money in a sack and take off."
>
> —NASCAR OFFICIAL JOE EPTON

The Marshall

Marshall Teague, a key participant in the December 1947 meetings that resulted in NASCAR's birth, was a Daytona Beach native who raced both stock cars and Indy-cars.

BIG BILL, BIG DREAMS

39

suggested: National Stock Car Racing Association and National Association of Stock Car Auto Racing (the "of" later became "for"). The first choice won on the first vote, but Vogt, who had suggested NASCAR, told the meeting that a group sanctioning races in Georgia already had the NSCRA name. There was a quick second vote, and, at about 3:30 in the afternoon, NASCAR was chosen.

Daytona Beach lawyer Louis Ossinsky, a France friend, agreed to arrange the legal paperwork for NASCAR's incorporation, a job that was completed on February 21, 1948. France, Tuthill, and Ossinsky were named as the stockholders. Promoter Ed Otto later would acquire shares, but France eventually bought full ownership of the corporation.

By the end of the Streamline Hotel meetings, France had designed a package that was agreeable to the men he had assembled. Many years later, Bobby Allison, one of NASCAR's leading drivers and a France combatant on more than one occasion, called France "probably the most personally forceful person I ever met. He just demanded that people support whatever the activity was he was involved in at that particular day and time. He had a way of demanding support without making people turn away. He wouldn't compromise. It would be 'No, we're going to do it my way, and you're going to help me.' He really had an unusual quality about him from that standpoint."

> "He had a way of demanding support without making people turn away. He wouldn't compromise."
>
> — DRIVER BOBBY ALLISON

In early 1948, NASCAR advertised "Competition memberships and associate memberships open to all persons who drive an automobile." Ten dollars bought a year's membership, membership card, car decal, membership pin, bulletins, and ten dollars worth of coupons, each good for fifty cents off race admission. NASCAR's first "office" was in the home of Bill and Anne France at 29 Goodall Avenue in Daytona Beach. Later the headquarters was moved to an office at 800 Main Street. "We used to cheer when the mail came in and we had a handful of memberships," said Dorothy Beech, who along with Judy Jones, worked in the NASCAR office in the early months and remains a part of the NASCAR family today.

"Dorothy acted as CFO," said Bill France, Jr. "She was the financial point of the organization and kept track of where monies came from and where they went. Judy Jones *was* the office, doing everything from answering the telephone, serving as receptionist, and most importantly, she was my father's secretary and ran the office when everyone was out on the road."

No one knew whether the new organization would succeed. Benny Kahn, an admirer of France, called it "a paper dream." *Speed Age* magazine was impressed by the meetings, however, calling the formation of the corporation "the most advanced step in a decade for the betterment of the auto racing sport" and referring to it as "the potentially mighty NASCAR."

The same issue of *Speed Age* included a short report on Fonty Flock being crowned champion of the 1947 National Championship Stock Car Circuit. That was now the past for France. The future held much promise. He was becoming Big Bill.

Getting started

Bill France (left) and NASCAR's first commissioner, E. G. "Cannonball" Baker (right) prepare for the start of a race with Harry Hartz. Opposite: NASCAR's first staff gathers outside the organization's first "official" office.

Over the years, the prices have changed, the colors have become more vivid, and the page counts have increased, but the concept of the racing souvenir program has stayed much the same: Give fans a look at the drivers, the teams, and the track for that particular weekend. Many programs from NASCAR's early years have increased dramatically in value and are prized by collectors. The sixth annual Firecracker 400 at Daytona, top, was held in 1964 and was one of seven NASCAR Winston Cup Series races won by legendary driver A. J. Foyt. The 1968 Daytona 500, the tenth running of NASCAR's biggest race, showcased up-and-coming Cale Yarborough, who won the event from the pole. The 1982 Busch Nashville 420 was won by Darrell Waltrip, who was driving for program cover boy Junior Johnson. An Atlanta 500 program featured Fred Lorenzen, who won four races at the Georgia track.

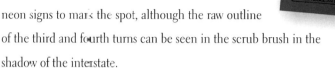

In early 1948, France announced a crowded schedule of forty races and offered the opinion that, "Stock car racing has boomed beyond anyone's wildest dreams, and I feel that we are in for another big year." NASCAR published and distributed its "1948 Rules and Specifications," a document that contained the organization's first logo, which featured a crossed pair of checkered flags and two winged cars. Oddly, the cars were pointed at each other.

Among the thirty-five listed rules:

   3. Foreign-manufactured cars will not be permitted.

   6. Stock bumpers and mufflers must be removed.

   13. Cars must be equipped with rear view mirror.

   18. Cars may be run with or without fan or generator.

Six days before NASCAR was officially incorporated, an anxious France held the first race under NASCAR sanction. It was a Modified event on the familiar Beach-Road course, and Red Byron, the Atlanta rocket, rolled home first.

France's Modified races featured older cars, usually 1930s models, with motors tweaked in every way imaginable by the mechanics of the day. The cars became NASCAR's first racers in large part because they were available. The impact of World War II was great on automobile manufacturers, and their production of new cars didn't reach optimum levels until years after the end of the war, leaving potential racers with what were, in a very real sense, "used" cars.

NASCAR sanctioned fifty-two races during that first year, and almost all were in the Southeast. A year later, the sanctioned total had grown to eighty-seven, and NASCAR's reach stretched to an event in Buffalo, New York.

France's simple but ultimately grand concept—that spectators would be more attracted to races that matched street sedans rather than the modified coupes that had dominated much of stock car racing in the years immediately before and after World War II—got its first test in Charlotte on that warm June day in 1949.

Charlotte Speedway, today only a memory, was located about twenty-five miles west of present-day Lowe's Motor Speedway, the 1.5-mile ultramodern facility that currently hosts

the NASCAR Winston Cup Series in its visits to the Charlotte area. Perhaps appropriately, Interstate 85, one of the nation's busiest expressways and a path for racing fans bound for Charlotte, Atlanta, Rockingham, Talladega, and other motorsports hot spots, slices through the site of the old track. There are no historical markers or neon signs to mark the spot, although the raw outline of the third and fourth turns can be seen in the scrub brush in the shadow of the interstate.

Here Bill France rolled the dice and came up a big winner. Although NASCAR had been established in the final weeks of 1947 and France had been promoting races for years before its incorporation, he didn't have the only game in town. There were other stock car racing organizations, some rough-edged, some promising. France saw that summer as the time to begin to separate himself from the rest, and he saw Strictly Stock as the vehicle.

He announced a 150-mile race for the Charlotte track and posted a five-thousand-dollar purse. The speedway had been in operation for a year but had run only Modified races. This would be its first big test, too, a sort of coming-out party for a ragged racetrack that suddenly found itself on the edge of history.

No one knew how many drivers would show up, how many spectators would be interested, how the cars would perform, if any would be running at day's end.

The second question—that of fan interest—was answered early. "There were fans here at 6 A.M. that day," said David Allison, son of Carl Allison, who owned the track. "They came from everywhere.

Year one

A crowd of more than twelve thousand, opposite, packed Charlotte Speedway in North Carolina for the first Strictly Stock race in June 1949. Visible in front of the grandstand at left is Lee Petty's Buick Roadmaster, which would crash about halfway through the race. NASCAR's first rule book, left, issued in 1948, included specifications for eligible car models and a list of officials. An entry blank, above, for the first Strictly Stock race at Charlotte carried NASCAR's first logo, featuring winged race cars aimed at each other.

Cars were parked as far as four miles away. People were trying to get in everywhere. We had people climbing trees to see. Daddy would crank up a chain saw and go over there. He wouldn't actually cut the trees down, but they would come out of them anyway."

On that day in Charlotte, estimates of the crowd ranged from twelve thousand to twenty-three thousand. People who were there place the number at around thirteen thousand, more than enough, certainly, to endorse France's new concept.

Then the race began. And the red clay of Charlotte was reassembled.

The big stockers, their engines booming, pounded around the three-quarter-mile track like a horde of buzz bombs, their bulks cutting deeper and deeper ruts into the rough surface. It was barely controlled chaos.

"It was so dusty that day that you would run by the grandstand, go all the way around the track, and come back and run through the dust you had stirred up the lap before," remembered Tim Flock, who arrived in Charlotte with no car to race, talked a visiting couple into using their new Oldsmobile 88, and finished fifth. "We took masking tape, probably a hundred rolls, and taped the bumpers and the chrome, trying to keep the rocks from really beating up the cars. But when the race was over, the front end was all beat up."

This was nothing new for dirt-track auto racing, of course. There were better tracks than the old Charlotte Speedway, and there were many worse. Old jalopies and battered coupes, many rescued from the despair of forgotten junkyards, had been circling these hard-clay bullrings for years. Racing virtually new showroom-clean automobiles ("cars you'd drive to church," as one driver once put it) on these barren landscapes was another matter entirely, an obvious point to France, who had envisioned what could be.

It was grand theater.

Before the first race, there were only minor concessions in car preparation. Drivers were allowed to reinforce wheels with metal plates because the extreme pressure on tires through the track's rough turns caused lugs to push through the wheels.

Safety equipment? The driver had only his common sense, and that element didn't appear to be in grand supply on this day.

"We were having a ball," said Flock. "Nobody had ever run those cars before. It was real close, and you couldn't get away from anybody. Guys didn't have safety belts. One guy drove with a truck inner tube around him. Another guy was tied in with a rope. The cars were pretty much just like they came from the dealer. No roll bars. No nothing. No one had ever run brand-new cars, and people came out just to see what in the world was going to happen."

Ned Jarrett, later a star racer himself and, still later, a commentator for televised racing broadcasts, was in the group anxious to experience this slice of history. "I was standing next to the fence at the start-finish line," he said. "I thought that was the place to be. All of a sudden, a car came down through there and a fan blade flew off and stuck in the wooden post right where I was leaning. I quickly figured out that was not the place to be."

Bob Flock led the day's first lap but parked his Hudson with engine trouble after only thirty-eight laps. Radiators erupted like geysers around the track as overheating problems nailed car after car. The top survivor of one of the wildest days in auto racing history was Glenn Dunnaway, who had motored over from nearby Gastonia, jumped in a Ford entered by Hubert Westmoreland, and dominated the last portion of the race. He finished three laps in front of Jim

The beginning

Cars with crudely painted numbers and headlights taped to limit damage from flying rocks and other debris circle Charlotte Speedway on June 19, 1949, in NASCAR's first Strictly Stock race.

Roper, whose entry into the event was certainly the most unlikely. A resident of Halstead, Kansas, Roper had decided to try this new form of racing only after reading about the event in a newspaper comic strip authored by cartoonist and racing fan Zack Mosley.

Despite a celebration by Dunnaway and Westmoreland, Roper drove home to Kansas with the day's first-place prize of two thousand dollars. A postrace inspection revealed that Westmoreland's 1947 Ford, a converted moonshine hauler, had been raced with altered rear springs. Known as bootlegger springs, they had been installed to support the heavy loads of liquor carried by the car. Dunnaway was disqualified, elevating Roper from second to first.

Roper, who had driven his 1949 Lincoln racer from Kansas—"nonstop," he said—didn't have transportation home because NASCAR officials removed the engine after the race for inspection. Mecklenburg Motors in Charlotte gave Roper a new engine, and NASCAR's first Strictly Stock winner was on his way home.

"I didn't find out I'd won until the next day," said Roper. "They disqualified Dunnaway after we had left the track. It was a very controversial race, but it was competitive, too. The track was rough. But back then most everything was dirt. You're going to have a hole or two. You couldn't race very hard and not have one or two in the racetrack."

> "We took masking tape, probably a hundred rolls, and taped the bumpers and the chrome, trying to keep the rocks from really beating up the cars."
> —DRIVER TIM FLOCK

The Charlotte race marked the debut of a scoring system NASCAR would use for decades to come. Joe Epton, the chief scorer, "borrowed" the system—and a scoring clock—from the American Motorcyclist Association. Scorers sitting on a flatbed truck in the infield used individual cards to record the clock time as each car passed the start-finish line. At race's end, the cards could be assembled in the proper order, and the clock numbers could be used to resolve disputes—at least, in theory. NASCAR's earlier scoring system was quite rudimentary. It consisted of Epton and another scorer, Harry Sink, sitting side by side, Sink yelling car numbers into Epton's ear as drivers roared by the start-finish line. "He smoked cigars," Epton remembered, "and it took me three days after a race to get the tobacco out of my ear."

Among those who didn't particularly enjoy the day in Charlotte was Lee Petty, a calculating, hard-nosed driver from Level Cross, North Carolina, who one day would be a NASCAR champion. Petty, who drove a delivery truck for a bakery, drove a Buick Roadmaster in the race and was rolling along in fine shape until an accident sent the car into a wild roll. The driver wasn't seriously hurt, but the car was crumpled. Petty, who with sons Richard and Maurice would later become key figures in one of racing's biggest success stories, hitchhiked home.

Payday

Above, Bill France Sr. presents driver Fonty Flock
(back row, center) with a check for finishing in
second place in driver points in the 1948 season,
the first year NASCAR awarded point fund money.
Checks presented to Robert "Red" Byron, opposite,
and Flock, were drawn on the First Atlantic
National Bank in Daytona. Women drivers also
have been on NASCAR pay sheets. Louise Smith,
right, was among NASCAR's pioneer female racers.

Day was done. Bill France's experiment was a financial, if not completely artistic, success.

There would be many laps to run. An endless highway awaited.

❦

Encouraged by the response at Charlotte, France quickly scheduled nine more Strictly Stock races for the 1949 season (although the last two, at Lakewood Park in Atlanta, weren't included in the championship point count).

The second race was held July 10 on the familiar Beach-Road course at Daytona. Red Byron won by taking the lead from Gober Sosebee six laps from the finish. Three women, Sara Christian, Louise Smith, and Ethel Mobley, ran in the event. Christian had become the series' first female participant in the Charlotte race, finishing fourteenth.

The series moved to Hillsboro, North Carolina, and the super fast and dangerous Occoneechee Speedway August 7, where Bob Flock prevailed before a crowd of more than seventeen thousand. Race four at Langhorne, Pennsylvania, a month later marked the first victory for Virginia dirt-track wizard Curtis Turner, who was starting a NASCAR career that would rise to legendary status. Other winners in that first season were Jack White, Lee Petty, Flock, and Byron.

When the point season ended October 16 at North Wilkesboro, North Carolina, Byron stood as the first Strictly Stock champion,

reaching the highlight of a remarkable career. Born in 1915 in Boulder, Colorado, Byron moved to Alabama in the 1930s and raced short tracks there. He raced on the beach at Daytona before joining the Army Air Corps in World War II. Flying in a B24 over the Aleutian Islands, Byron was hit by Japanese fire, downing his plane and crippling his left leg. He was hospitalized for about two years.

Byron returned to racing after the war. Although he had limited use of his left leg, he was able to drive by strapping his foot to a harness that tied it to the clutch. Despite the handicap, he won NASCAR's Modified championship in 1948 before driving Raymond Parks's Oldsmobiles in 1949 to the first title in what would later become the NASCAR Winston Cup Series.

Parks described Byron as "a quiet man who didn't have too much to say." Much the same could be said of Parks, a shy person who enjoyed the racing honors he would receive late in life (hall of fame inductions, for example) but wasn't too thrilled about the public goings-on that accompanied them.

Parks, who still has the championship trophy in his Atlanta office, enjoyed the moment but, of course, didn't have an inkling of where all this would lead. "I didn't think it was that significant right then," he said. "I was always glad to win, and winning that [championship] was something, too. But at that time I didn't realize it would become as big as it has and that being the first one to win the championship would mean that much."

Victory photos of Byron show him wearing a crash helmet, a big cigar, and a pound or two of dirt collected from the tracks he had conquered. "Most of the time Red had a cigar in his mouth," Parks said. "His driving style? The first part of a race he'd kind of sit back. About halfway, he took off. He wouldn't stay too far back, but he wouldn't get out front right away, either. He won a good many races that way."

In major league stock car racing's first season, Red Byron spread more dust than the rest of his contemporaries and forever will be known as NASCAR's first champion.

ill France Sr. wasn't the only dreamer roaming motorsports back roads in the 1940s.

If people scoffed at France's ideas of corralling wayward stock car racers into a legitimate organization, they were almost hysterical when they heard Harold Brasington's plan. A resident of tiny Darlington, South Carolina, and owner of a heavy-equipment business, Brasington returned from a trip to Indianapolis Motor Speedway with the idea to build a giant, paved racetrack in the tobacco country near his home.

Never mind that there would be no major highway or large town near the track. Never mind that most southern stockers had never raced on an asphalt surface. Never mind that speeds on such a track could prove problematic.

Brasington didn't listen to those who didn't believe. Selling other local businessmen on his idea over a period of years, and selling stock along downtown Darlington streets to somewhat puzzled residents, he raised the money and began building the track. To say he had something less than a master plan is to understate the matter.

The shape of the South's first major speedway is unlike any other motorsports facility in the world. Brasington had to engineer around a fish pond to honor the wishes of the man who owned the land where the track was located.

FROM
DIRT TO DAYTONA

"Big Bill" France inspects the asphalt laid down for what became NASCAR's fastest speedway, Daytona International Speedway. Opposite: Dale Earnhardt (No. 3) and Jeff Gordon speed along the track's banking under the lights of Daytona International Speedway during the first night race held on October 17, 1998.

A huge field of seventy-five cars started the first Southern 500 at Darlington Raceway, September 4, 1950. In the front row were Gober Sosebee (No. 51), Jimmy Thompson (No. 25), and Curtis Turner (No. 41).

Sherman Ramsey traded seventy acres of his Darlington farm, about a mile from town on the Darlington-Hartsville highway, to Brasington for stock in the track. When Brasington broke ground for the speedway December 13, 1949, he did so with an obstacle. When Ramsey made the agreement, he told Brasington that he wanted to preserve the small minnow pond on the land. Thus, Darlington's turns are shaped differently, for Brasington's land-moving equipment had to swerve a bit to keep the pond intact. It seemed like a small thing then, but it gave the speedway one of the strangest footprints—that of a pear—in all of racing. The first and second turns are tight, while the third and fourth are much more sweeping.

Brasington cut the track in a 1.25-mile oval, leaving little banking. (The surface would be changed three times, eventually gaining more banking and expanding to the present 1.366 miles.) Working long hours (often roaming the property by himself on earth-moving machinery), Brasington, amazingly, completed the track in less than a year.

Darlington's arrival set the stage for one of NASCAR's first major crossroads. Brasington had made a deal with the Central States Racing Association based in Columbus, Ohio, to sanction his first race, and he scheduled it for September 4, 1950 (Labor Day). But CSRA officials had trouble collecting entries for the race. Under the gun, Brasington met with Bill France, now well into his second season of Grand National (his new name for the

Strictly Stock division) racing. After touring the construction site, France agreed to cosanction the event with CSRA, and Brasington soon had a field overflowing with cars.

Although final work on the speedway was not completed, teams and drivers began arriving in Darlington in late August for the five-hundred-mile race, some still wondering if the whole thing was real. Stockers had never run five hundred miles, after all, and there was some question that the cars could last through a race of that length.

France and other officials, recognizing the uniqueness of the event, decided to go the extra mile in the publicity department, stretching qualifying over fifteen days. The fastest five drivers each day made the field, which, by race day, reached the staggering total of seventy-five. As impressive as the number was the quality of the starting grid. Lining up in the three-abreast start were, among others, Fireball Roberts, Red Byron, Lee Petty, Cotton Owens, Tim Flock, Bob Flock, Fonty Flock, Jack Smith, Curtis Turner, Marshall Teague, and Buck Baker—some of the best stock car drivers of that, or any, era.

None of them knew what to expect. The first Southern 500 was truly an experimental affair.

"It looked like a bunch of New York taxicabs when they threw that flag," said Tim Flock. "The track was dusty. Man, you couldn't see going into that first turn after the first or second lap. It was just mayhem."

The unpredictable nature of the spectacle attracted a massive crowd to the speedway. Thousands poured into the Darlington area the day before the race, and many more arrived on race morning. The rural roads in the area were the scene of a colossal traffic jam as a crowd estimated at twenty-thousand tried to find the way to ticket sellers who were issuing tickets for five dollars a customer.

Dawn of Darlington

NASCAR official Bill Tuthill (holding microphone) interviews Darlington Raceway founder Harold Brasington with first Southern 500 winner Johnny Mantz (second from right) and NASCAR commissioner Cannonball Baker. Opposite: Mantz receives his trophy.

Few of the drivers, the vast majority of whom had never raced on asphalt, could have predicted the day's most taxing problem: tire wear. The impressive speed of the cars—Turner had won the pole at 82.034 mph—and their headlong runs through the turns ate tires. Blowouts were the order of the day.

"We parked the Lincoln [driven by Harold Kite] because it burned up tires so bad we couldn't keep tires on it," said car owner Bud Moore, who also had a Mercury driven by Joe Eubanks in the race. "I remember Red Vogt had a Cadillac that Red Byron was driving, and they used seventy-five tires on it. About everybody ran out. We went out in the infield and jacked up spectators' cars and took the tires off them."

Flock said racing on the new asphalt surface, dusted with sand, was "like running on sandpaper."

Chaos reigned, in part because of the size of the field. "When the race got started, there were cars everywhere," Moore said. "Just imagine taking the field we've got now [typically forty-three cars] and doubling it. The track was full." And the drama and confusion in the pits were heightened by the fact that there was no wall between the track and the stalls in which drivers stopped their cars for service. Tire changes were made with cars zipping by only a few feet away.

Early in the event, most drivers tried to race on the inside, flatter part of the track. It was, after all, the shortest way around,

> "About everybody ran out. We went out in the infield and jacked up spectators' cars and took the tires off them."
>
> — Car owner Bud Moore

and some were unsure what would happen on the banking. As the race dragged on, many discovered that driving higher on the banking gave more life to their tires.

Hershel McGriff, who raced across the full fifty years of NASCAR's first half-century, started thirty-fourth in that first 500. "One thing I remember at the start is the screeching of the tires," he said. "They made so much noise. Most of us were running on the flat part of the track, and I had a lot of tire trouble like everybody else." He pitted so often, McGriff said, that he eventually jumped out of the car during pit stops to assist with tire changes.

It was a long, long day, one of the most astounding in NASCAR history. The race lasted six hours and thirty-eight minutes.

"It was strictly chaos," said Richard Petty, who watched from the infield as his father Lee competed. "We were here for a week or two. It took forever and ever. We'd wear out tires and motors just trying to get qualified and ready for the race. It wasn't anything for people to bounce off the fences during the race."

One of the quirks of the first 500 was that its winner, Johnny Mantz, a successful midget racer who had had experience in the Indianapolis 500, also was its slowest qualifier. Instead of roaring along at top speed every lap, Mantz approached the race with an intelligent game plan, managing his speed at about 75 mph with a stopwatch and trying to run consistent, if slower, laps. He was passed repeatedly, but he also had much better luck with tire wear, and he rolled along while others made return trips to the pits for new rubber.

By lap fifty, Mantz had the lead, and he stayed there the rest of the day, finishing a full nine laps in front of second-place Roberts.

A madman comes home first

Johnny "Madman" Mantz used smart tire strategy to avoid repetitive pit stops and win the first Southern 500. At left, Mantz (right) is congratulated by Fireball Roberts (left) and Red Byron.

Almost immediately, stories began circulating about Mantz's victory. Some said he used special racing tires; others said his car's engine was too big. The complete story probably will never be known. The winning Plymouth had been purchased in the days before the race by Bill France, Curtis Turner, and Alvin Hawkins. They put it in mechanic Hubert Westmoreland's hands for the race and he prepared it for Mantz, who had become friends with France and Turner when the trio drove in a Mexican road race earlier that year. Questions about the car's status persisted after the 500, but it was approved after a postrace inspection that lasted until the early hours of the next day.

Despite the controversy, stock car racers had proven that they—and their rides—could last five hundred miles, establishing a key benchmark in France's struggle to push his organization forward.

In the Darlington infield, Bill France Jr., then seventeen, was working, too. He sold snow cones for ten cents each.

❦

The early years of stock car racing, even into the period when Bill France and NASCAR began to provide a framework of organization to the sport, were rough, unrefined, and dangerous. The cars had few safety enhancements. Many of the tracks were so primitive that cars literally bounced along their surfaces, moving from one rut to the next. Starting fields were volatile mixes of devil-may-care moonshiners, adventurers who longed for nothing more than to sit behind a powerful engine and run unbridled into the wild blue yonder,

Well into the 1950s, drivers were still racing cars that they had driven to the track. The concept of towing cars evolved slowly.

and accomplished drivers who had won before and hoped to win again.

So, what was the strategy at the start of a hundred-lapper on some obscure dirt bullring in the Carolinas on a summer Saturday night? "You just mashed the pedal to the floor and went," said Buck Baker, one of NASCAR's early stars. "Driving the cars was like having two mad bulls with one set of harnesses on them and you didn't know where they were going. Some of the time you could see; most of the time you couldn't. You picked out a landmark like a parked car someplace around the track to know when to turn.

"I loved to drive fast, and I had a place to do it. That was my thing. The driving was more fun than the competition. It didn't make a lot of difference to me where I finished or who won the race as long as I got to run."

He and most of the other barnstormers of the early years ran wild and free without much regard for safety. "My seat belt was an old plow line," Baker said. "I had a steering wheel break on me at the Charlotte fairgrounds once, and I drove with a pair of vise grips the rest of the race. Just clamped them down on the car and turned with the grips. It didn't go as fast as normal, but I finished the race."

Well into the 1950s, drivers were still racing cars that they had driven to the track. The concept of towing cars—and, later, hauling them in trucks and transporters—evolved slowly.

"I had a moonshine car that we started fixing on a Monday to go to race at Darlington," remembered Junior Johnson. "We went down on Tuesday and qualified and won the race. I drove the car back home. We took the headlights out and put beefed-up tires on it. There weren't a lot of major changes because what you would do to a car to race was about what you'd do to run moonshine, anyway."

Racing with wild abandon

In Buck Baker's day, left, safety equipment was just one area of innovation that had not been finessed when he drove in the dirt bullrings of the Carolinas.

Extra passenger

A broken leg kept Ralph Earnhardt out from behind the
wheel but still close to the camaraderie NASCAR races
offered. Here he jokes around with (clockwise from his left)
Bobby Isaac, Ned Jarrett, and Richard Petty.

NASCAR Winston Cup Series cars have raced from sea to shining sea, from Maine to California, in most of the fifty states, twice north of the border (in Canada), and even across the Pacific (in Japan).

At more than 150 sites, on dirt, asphalt, concrete, and sand; at airports, football stadiums, and baseball fields; on ovals, rectangles, circles, and road courses, the green flag has been waved over starting fields of stock cars bearing the NASCAR badge.

The vast majority of the tracks that have hosted NASCAR Winston Cup races are no longer on the schedule for one obvious reason—the season's length. The 1999 schedule had room for thirty-four point races and two special events—thirty-six racing weekends in a fifty-two-weekend year at twenty-one locations. Quite a few short tracks dropped off the schedule in 1972 when the season was streamlined so that teams wouldn't be racing two and

three times in a single week. Other tracks—some tiny and out-of-date, others huge and majestic—no longer exist because the land upon which they were built was judged to be better real estate for other projects, such as shopping centers, industrial parks, and highways.

Thus, the series that is modern NASCAR Winston Cup racing was built on a crazy quilt of playing fields. Only one of the tracks on the original 1949 schedule—Martinsville Speedway in Virginia—remains on the modern schedule. Many others hosted one or two or many races but fell victim to size limitations, scheduling problems, location, or simply the passing of the years and were removed from the NASCAR Winston Cup schedule.

Among those tracks with a checkered past:

Soldier Field, Chicago. Yes, they raced stock cars in the same stadium where the Bears and Packers clash. A NASCAR Winston Cup race was held on a half-mile oval inside the stadium in 1956.

Las Vegas Park Speedway. A one-mile dirt track in Vegas, it brought the NASCAR Winston Cup Series west before the sparkling new Las Vegas Motor Speedway. Later torn down to make way for hotel construction, the track hosted the series in 1955.

Raleigh Speedway. Located near North Carolina's capital city, this one-mile paved track became NASCAR's first lighted superspeedway in the 1950s.

Before its time

Ontario Motor Speedway in California opened in 1970 and was regarded as one of the finest motorsports facilities of the period. It was torn down only a decade later, however, because the property was needed for commercial development.

Ontario Motor Speedway. One of the most modern and best-engineered tracks in the world, this 2.5-mile track had a bright but brief life. Opened in 1970 as a near-replica of Indianapolis Motor Speedway, Ontario lasted for a decade before it was demolished in favor of commercial development. The new California Speedway is located near the Ontario site.

North Wilkesboro Speedway. More than a few longtime racing fans shed a tear when Wilkesboro, a NASCAR charter track and the competition home of the legendary Junior Johnson, dropped off the NASCAR Winston Cup circuit in 1996. Located in the Brushy Mountains of western North Carolina, the track hosted some barnburner races over its half-century.

Linden, New Jersey, Airport. NASCAR put together airport runways here in 1954 to run the first NASCAR Winston Cup Series road race. Oddly enough, it was won by a Jaguar. Al Keller scored the only NASCAR Winston Cup win in a foreign car.

Langhorne Speedway. A wicked one-mile dirt track that formed almost a perfect circle, Langhorne opened in Pennsylvania in the 1920s and ran NASCAR Winston Cup Series races from 1949 to 1957.

Occoneechee Speedway. Located near Hillsboro, North Carolina, Occoneechee was a narrow and fast one-mile dirt oval that demanded the best from drivers. "It was a nervy sort of track," said Junior Johnson. "You had to know what you were doing there. I loved it." The track left the tour in 1968.

McCormick Field. Located in Asheville, North Carolina, McCormick was built for baseball but hosted the NASCAR Winston Cup Series in 1958 on a quarter-mile track that was carved into the baseball field.

Bowman-Gray Stadium. Bowman-Gray, like Greenville-Pickens in South Carolina, Hickory in North Carolina, and South Boston in Virginia, is a classic southern short track that no longer hosts NASCAR Winston Cup Series racing but schedules other NASCAR-sanctioned events. Bowman-Gray is located in Winston-Salem, North Carolina.

Part of the past

North Wilkesboro Speedway, left, in its dirt-track days, was removed from the NASCAR Winston Cup Series schedule after the 1996 season. Located in the Brushy Mountains of North Carolina, North Wilkesboro was considered the "home track" for nearby resident Junior Johnson. Above: Bowman-Gray Stadium, a quarter-mile oval, left the NASCAR Winston Cup Series in 1971 but still hosts weekly racing.

Although larger-than-life figures like Tim Flock and Curtis Turner came to dominate headlines as NASCAR moved through the 1950s, the man who ruled the decade from a performance standpoint was a Sanford, North Carolina, farmer who happened to see a race in Greensboro, figured he could do as well as the drivers in it, and set a course to meet that

goal. Herb Thomas, who was sort of the opposite of flamboyant, would become the most successful—if not the most publicized—of NASCAR's early drivers.

Thomas raced from 1950 to 1956. Over that short span, he won 48 races in 230 starts, a percentage of 20.8, within an eyelash of Tim Flock's all-time record of 21.1. Along the way, Thomas became the first driver to win the Grand National championship twice (1951 and '53) and easily could have won it several other times. He also was the first three-time winner of the Southern 500. "I could win [at Darlington]," Thomas said. "It was the first paved track I had ever been on, but I liked it."

Ray Fox Sr., who built cars for Thomas, called him "a fantastic driver. He knew how to take care of cars. About all the tracks were

dirt back then and were rough. But he was very patient."

Thomas drove to the 1953 championship in his Hudson Hornets, described as "Fabulous" in huge letters painted on their sides. The monster cars would become big hits of the racing 1950s, boosting showroom sales considerably. A Hudson magazine ad promoting the Hornet used this selling point: "Winner of more stock-car events than all other makes combined!"

NASCAR added a Short Track division to its menu in 1951 and, a year later, expanded to include a Speedway Division for Indy-type cars. Neither proved successful over the long haul. NASCAR's brief fling with Indy-cars ended after only seven races, with Buck Baker winning the championship. The sanctioning body also continued its popular Modified and Sportsman series, providing plenty of action for drivers who didn't have the money or inclination to chase the top division. Among the Sportsman aces was Ralph Earnhardt, father of future NASCAR Winston Cup champion Dale Earnhardt. Ralph Earnhardt, called "absolutely the toughest race driver I ever ran against" by Ned Jarrett, won the Sportsman championship in 1956 with thirty-four victories although he never won a Grand National race.

The Grand Nationals continued to gather steam, moving to new areas of the country and producing new stars. The series' first road race was held June 13, 1954, at Linden, New Jersey, on an airport course. Al Keller won in a Jaguar, garnering the only victory by a foreign car in NASCAR Winston Cup Series history.

Early successes

NASCAR's short-lived Speedway Division put Indy-type cars on tracks that were traditionally stock car–oriented, as in this 1952 battle at Darlington Raceway, above. Herb Thomas, left, was the first driver to win two Grand National championships and came within an eyelash of Tim Flock's all-time record. Opposite: Flock drove one of the few four-door race cars to be used before the introduction of the 1999 Ford Taurus.

Kiekhaefer's cornucopia

Millionaire businessman Carl Kiekhaefer introduced team racing in the early 1950s. Kiekhaefer reinforced unity through matching uniforms, cars, and transporter trucks that revolutionized the sport and advertised his Mercury Outboards. Tim Flock, opposite, drove for Kiekhaefer.

Tim Flock described the competition in the groundbreaking years of the early 1950s as intense. "When they dropped the flags back then, it was dog eat dog. We weren't worried about points. We were worried about making enough money to take home to feed the kids."

At that task, Flock was more successful than most. From the very first Strictly Stock race in Charlotte, he showed the skill, flair, and daring of a star. Born in Fort Payne, Alabama, and Hollywood handsome, Flock grew up in a family of daredevils (his father was a tightrope walker and his brothers and sister raced) and showed no fear in the often calamitous early days of an emerging sport. Off the track, he drove an Orange Crush truck and an Atlanta taxi.

Flock won the Grand National championship in 1952 and 1955, clinching the '52 title with his car on its roof after an accident at West Palm Beach, Florida. Flock had no racing plans for the '55 season, having walked away from the sport in anger after being disqualified at a Daytona Beach-Road course race in 1954. He spent most of that year running a service station in Atlanta and returned to Daytona Beach the following February as a spectator. A fortuitous turn of events placed Flock on the beach at the same time as stock car racing newcomer Carl Kiekhaefer, a man who would bring revolutionary ideas to the sport. He also brought a big white Chrysler 300 to Flock.

"I was standing there with a bunch of people, watching cars test on the beach," Flock said. "All of a sudden, this big Chrysler 300 came by. I looked at my buddies and said, 'Man, if I had that car I'd win the race here again this year.' Standing about three people from me was a guy from Orlando who was a Mercury outboard dealer. He said, 'I know the man who owns that car. Would you like to meet him?'"

The man was Kiekhaefer, a millionaire businessman who came into racing like a bright comet, conquered almost all comers, and was gone almost as suddenly.

Detroit manufacturers had begun supplying teams with "severe usage kits" during the 1953 season, putting high-performance parts and more safety equipment into the sport. But Kiekhaefer, a Wisconsin native, is given credit for accelerating the

factories' interest in stock car racing. His approach to racing—he wanted to win every race and spent more than enough money to do so—was like none before him. In one event late in the 1955 season, he owned or sponsored seven cars.

Kiekhaefer settled for nothing less than perfection. His mechanics wore identical white uniforms (a first for a sport that hadn't exactly emphasized fashion), and his cars and equipment arrived at tracks in shiny new trucks. He introduced "team" racing to NASCAR and was the first to make serious use of the sport in promotion, advertising his Mercury boat motors on the sides of his cars and transporter trucks ("See The Colorful Kiekhaefer Mercury Outboards"). He also enforced some unusual team rules, such as demanding curfews for his mechanics and keeping his drivers and their wives separated in different wings of motels on the nights before races.

Fireball Roberts finished first in that race on the beach, but he was disqualified, and Flock, who drove for Kiekhaefer, discovered the next morning at breakfast that he had been awarded the victory. It was the beginning of a remarkable run with Kiekhaefer. Flock won a whopping eighteen races for him in 1955 but left the owner early in the 1956 season.

While Kiekhaefer made big noise in 1955 and '56, the '55 season also saw the first big splash by Junior Johnson, who won five races in 1955 and challenged Turner in the category of "finish first or not at all."

Also among the heroes in that first group of pioneer racers was Lee Petty, who would start one of the most extraordinary family stories in auto racing history. Working from an old reaper shed with a dirt floor on his property in Level Cross, North Carolina, Petty joined in with the first wave of dirt-track racers. A steady driver who seldom failed to finish a race (he became known as Mr. Consistency), he won the series championship in 1954 and '58. Petty Enterprises expanded from the open-sided reaper

two convertible races that season, but Bob Welborn won the championship, the first of three titles he would win in the division. Although Darlington Raceway continued to hold convertible races into the 1960s, the division officially folded in 1959. For a short run, however, the convertibles gave fans a unique view of the racer at work. "One of the things people really liked about the convertibles was that at most racetracks they could see you plain as day in there," said driver Jack Smith. "They could see you work your hands and react to everything."

Another series that sprang up in the 1950s continues today. The Pacific Coast Late Model circuit, now the NASCAR Winston West Series, was born in 1954 when NASCAR came west. Among the current top NASCAR drivers produced by the Winston West Series are Ron Hornaday, Kevin Harvick, and Rick Carelli. Two-time NASCAR Winston Cup Series winner Derrike Cope and Roush Racing driver Chad Little are among Winston Cup drivers who boosted their careers with Winston West activity.

shed to a massive racing business that fields vehicles for three NASCAR divisions. Through NASCAR's first half-century, the Petty Enterprises name stood for quality through four generations of family racers.

The 1956 season saw Kiekhaefer cars win twenty-one of the first twenty-five races, including a stunning sixteen straight. When Flock left the team early in the season, Herb Thomas signed on, joining Speedy Thompson and Buck

> "One of the things people really liked about the convertibles was that they could see you plain as day in there."
> — DRIVER JACK SMITH

The Detroit factories' increasing interests in stock car racing made a U-turn in 1957 after a recommendation by the Automobile Manufacturers Association that the car builders distance themselves from motorsports. The fac-

Baker as Kiekhaefer pilots. But Thomas tired of Kiekhaefer and returned to his own team in July.

The carousel of driver changes within Kiekhaefer's team impacted the flow of the championship race that season. Thomas led Baker in points in the season's final weeks, and Kiekhaefer leased a track in Shelby, North Carolina, to add a race to the schedule (not an uncommon practice in those days) in late October, giving Baker another chance to gain points. Thompson and Thomas crashed about halfway through the race, and Baker got the win.

When the 1956 season ended, Kiekhaefer dropped out of the sport, disappointed with the adverse reaction fans had shown to his team's run to the championship.

NASCAR added convertible racing to its divisions in 1956 after a merger with the Society of Autosports and Fellowship Education (SAFE), a midwestern sanctioning body. Curtis Turner proved to be particularly adept at cruising in the ragtops. He won twenty-

tories wouldn't be away for long, however, having learned the value of associating themselves with winning race teams. In the summer of 1957, driver-mechanic Ralph Moody and Californian John Holman formed Holman-Moody to absorb Ford's huge stockpile of racing equipment. Their partnership would become synonymous with the Ford name in stock car racing.

As the 1950s decade moved toward its close, the face of NASCAR racing was changing. In 1950, the Grand National schedule included seventeen dirt races and one asphalt event. By 1958, the numbers were almost equal—twenty-six dirt, twenty-four paved. Many dirt tracks across the Southeast switched to asphalt in the late '50s, and others would follow in the next decade.

Fast for Ford

A 1957 meeting brought together Ford racing hotshots (left to right) Curtis Turner, factory racing director Pete DePaolo, Fireball Roberts, and John Holman.

Rolling ragtops

Joe Weatherly (No. 12) and Lee Petty test their skills in convertibles during a 1958 race on the Daytona Beach sand.

Sands of time

Above: Bill France Sr. (right) and newspaperman Henry McLemore pose with a promotional vehicle advertising racing on the beach. Below, June Cleveland (No. 55) churns along the beach portion of the course in front of Red Byron in a race in 1950.

It was a race course unique in the annals of motorsports.

Not too often, after all, does this sort of quote emerge from drivers: "I've seen guys come out of the south turn there late in the race with the tide coming in and slide out into the water."

That was the late Joe Littlejohn, a pioneer stock car driver and promoter, talking about racing on the old Daytona Beach-Road course, the forerunner to the giant Daytona International Speedway and one of the bedrocks of NASCAR racing.

The course—actually there were three, each of a different length—was both a substitute and an amalgamation. Land-speed racers had plied the sands of Ormond Beach and Daytona Beach since near the turn of the twentieth century, but they deserted Florida in the mid-1930s for the bigger landscape of the Bonneville Salt Flats in Utah. That left Daytona without a motorsports game to call its own so, in 1936, city officials plotted a new offensive. Combining the straight stretch of the hard-packed beach sand and the parallel two-lane Highway A1A, they formed a temporary course that sent drivers racing north on the beach, turning left onto the two-lane asphalt highway, then roaring down

the pavement to turn left again and return to the sand. The longest, last, and most popular course was 4.1 miles in length and was located on the south end of the beach, near Ponce Inlet.

For most of three decades, ending in 1958, the Beach-Road course gave racing fans some of the most spectacular and wildly unusual action in motorsports history.

Cars hit the sandy ruts in the turns and overturned. Drivers overestimated the speed needed to make the south turn, rolled over dunes, and wound up in a junkpile of cars. Occasionally, cars spun and flipped and landed in the surf. And several races were shortened because the tide rolled in and turned the race course into water.

"It was a tricky place to have a race because you always had to schedule the start as the tide was just about all the way out so that the beach would be as wide as possible," racing historian Bob Latford said. "Then you hoped to run it quick enough before the tide came back in. Sometimes, offshore winds pushed the tide back in too quick and the race had to be called short."

Imagine: A race called because of ocean.

"The beach was different from anything else you could tackle," said driver Junior Johnson, who tackled virtually every racing surface he could find. "Coming down the beach heading into the north turn was an art, sort of like gliding an airplane. You started a quarter mile from the turn and you came in off the water. You turned that thing sideways two-tenths of a mile before you got to the turn.

"It was a very, very nervy racetrack. You didn't just run down there and cut the wheel. You had to have a pretty good knack for what you were doing.

Going down the asphalt the other way, it was just the opposite. You go down there, stop, and turn left. At about thirty to thirty-five miles per hour."

Highway A1A was only twenty-two feet from side to side; drivers who raced there say it wasn't wide enough to promote a lot of passing.

And the turns. They quickly became traps for drivers who didn't know what to expect.

"Both the entry to the north turn and the south turn exit would eventually get chewed up," said Latford, who worked in various jobs at beach races. "The tires would eat into the sand. It wasn't a quagmire, but more a bog of sand. A lot of cars would end up getting stalled."

There was more than one reason for wanting to be riding in first place in a beach race. Everybody driving behind the leader got a windshield full of wet beach sand, promoting the use of what has been a missing vehicle piece for most of NASCAR history: the windshield wiper.

"The sand stayed wet all the time," remembered Littlejohn. "You were always throwing it on the windshields of the other cars. It would eventually sandblast the front end of the car. You couldn't see to drive the car home at night after the race. If you were in a pack during the race, you couldn't see where you were going, unless, of course, you were in front." Not surprisingly, drivers used the sand as a weapon, intentionally sending a spray onto other cars to gain every possible advantage.

Some drivers carried small mops in their cars. During opportune moments, they reached out and cleaned their windshields.

Although the nearby presence of the Atlantic Ocean obviously was a hazard, it also held a benefit. Drivers

whose cars were overheating sometimes ran out into the shallow surf to let the ocean water cool their radiators.

Despite the elements and the general uncertainty of racing on the beach, the course was popular among drivers. Entry lists usually were very long (a Modified race once attracted 137 cars). Beach winner Cotton Owens said wins there were particularly sweet. "Those wins were great because of all the competition," he said. "It was something else to go down there and outrun so many cars."

The late Tim Flock called the beach course "the most beautiful race course that ever was."

Old film of the beach races shows spectators standing perilously close to the action. Sand dunes between the beach part of the course and the highway provided a good, if risky, vantage point. And some spectators were more curious than others. "As the cars came up the beach, they'd step out so they could see around the person beside them," Latford said. "They kept moving out and created a hazard."

Other fans watched the races from boats parked beyond the surf line. Bill France Sr., the promoter who turned the beach races into a successful venture, had some problems with spectators entering the race area without paying. This led to the erection of ominous signs along the sand dunes: *Beware of Rattlesnakes*.

Growth along the shore eventually forced the end of the beach racing era. With more and more hotels being built beside the ocean and traffic increasing in the course area, plans were made to build a new racing facility several miles west of the beach. Daytona International Speedway became a reality in 1959, a year after the final run on the sand.

NASCAR President Bill France Jr., who assisted his father at most of the beach races, called the course "pretty spectacular with the ocean in the background. It would have made a nice movie."

France, though, wasn't distressed to see NASCAR races move from the beach to the new speedway. "You had no control over the conditions there," he said. "It was a nightmare."

Beach boys

Among the top drivers of the beach racing era were (left to right) Billy Myers, Buck Baker, Jim Paschal, Lee Petty, and Speedy Thompson.

On July 12, 1958, in a one-hundred-mile convertible race in Columbia, South Carolina, the NASCAR ranks picked up a new driver. Tall, lanky, and personable, twenty-one-year-old Richard Petty wheeled a Petty Enterprises Oldsmobile to a sixth-place finish.

He would be heard from again.

By the mid-1950s, it was evident that the days of racing on the Beach-Road course at Daytona were numbered. Hotel and business construction was crowding the area, and soon it would be logistically impossible to stage races on the combination beach-asphalt course. Over a period of years, Bill France Sr. worked deal after deal, twisted arms, begged favors and generally talked his way into the building of Daytona International Speedway, a 2.5-mile track that replaced the beach course and revolutionized stock car racing.

From the beginning, France had big ideas for Daytona. He wanted it at least as big as Indianapolis Motor Speedway—and faster. He wanted a unique tri-oval shape along the frontstretch, a touch that he guessed—correctly—would improve sight lines for fans sitting in the main grandstands. He wanted something his sport didn't have: a racing palace.

The speedway site, adjacent to the Daytona Beach airport, wasn't exactly pristine property. "There were three or four swamps in there," said Bill France Jr., who worked at the site almost every day during the construction process. "Part of it was pretty rough. I had to rent a mule one day to get some trees out of there."

The speedway's construction costs went beyond $2 million. With sales of stock in the new International Speedway Corporation and loans, France still needed more money—he put up his house as collateral—to cover expenses in the speedway's early years.

But France's vision was fulfilled. And the stock car racers who had been following his lead for a decade filed into this mammoth new facility to take a look at their future. The speeds were huge, but so was the track.

"Daytona was bigger and wider than anything we had run on," said driver Ned Jarrett, "and it just didn't feel like you were running that fast. It was sort of like going down the interstate at seventy-five miles per hour. It doesn't feel like you're going that fast, but you get on a two-lane road out in the country and go seventy-five, and it feels like you're literally flying."

To be sure, NASCAR had moved off the two-lane.

The first Daytona 500 at the new track was run February 22, 1959. If France needed a spectacle to christen his baby, the drivers provided one. The race was so exciting it lasted for three days. Well, sort of.

The five hundred miles swept past quickly. Remarkably, there were no caution flags, despite the fact that this sort of racing on a high-banked, very long oval was new to the competitors. At day's end, the race for the win was between Lee Petty in an Oldsmobile and Johnny Beauchamp in a Thunderbird. The finish was one of the closest in racing history. Petty got there first, but there was initial confusion over which driver was the winner. France named Beauchamp the "unofficial" winner, and he got the trophy and the first visit to a Daytona victory lane. France and other officials studied still photographs and film of the finish for three days before reversing the decision and awarding the victory to Petty.

France phoned Petty, who was staying at a Daytona Beach motel, with the news. He wasn't particularly surprised, Petty would say later, because he had known all along that he had won.

Thus began a long and lasting tie-in between the Petty name and Daytona. This was only the first moment of what would be a long-running drama.

JACKSON

Five mph on the backstretch

Bill France Jr., opposite, now president of NASCAR, operates a compactor during construction of the Daytona International Speedway backstretch in 1958. Unusual construction techniques were needed to build the steep banking in the turns at Daytona, above. At left, former Speedway director Spike Briggs, Bill France Sr., and former Speedway vice president Muse Womack (left to right) check construction of one of the now-famous twin tunnels that lead to the track infield.

Prior to the opening of Daytona International Speedway, top, in February 1959, NASCAR Winston Cup Series racing had been largely a sport contested on compact landscapes— tracks of about one-half mile in length, most with dirt surfaces. Daytona changed that scenario forever. Charlotte Motor Speedway, bottom, (CMS, now Lowe's Motor Speedway) followed Daytona. Driver Curtis Turner and Charlotte racing promoter Bruton Smith joined forces and broke ground for CMS July 29, 1959, five months after the first Daytona 500. Other large facilities followed. Atlanta International Raceway, now known as Atlanta Motor Speedway, opened July 31, 1960, and Marchbanks Speedway, a 1.4-mile track in Hanford, California, also came on board that year. North Carolina Motor Speedway joined the circuit in 1965. Later in the 1960s, other big tracks would come on line. Michigan International Speedway opened in 1968 and held its first NASCAR Winston Cup race the following year. Texas World Speedway near College Station also welcomed NASCAR in 1969 but left the NASCAR Winston Cup Series schedule in 1981, and Dover Downs International Speedway became another new stop in 1969. Talladega Superspeedway, middle photos and opposite, the biggest of the bunch at 2.66 miles, opened in 1969 as Alabama International Motor Speedway, taking the concept of high-speed racing to yet another tier. Las Vegas Motor Speedway was one of NASCAR's new stops in the 1990s.

SHORT TRACKS

Short-track racing is the NASCAR Winston Cup Series' most visible link to its storied past. At tracks like Martinsville, top and middle, Richmond, opposite, and Bristol, bottom, the echoes of fierce battles between Turner and Johnson, Jarrett and Petty, Allison and Yarborough can be heard. At these asphalt and concrete monuments to the way things were forty years ago, NASCAR's modern-day racers engage in close quarters, heavy-contact racing that, by definition, isn't a part of superspeedway competition. After a race on the Martinsville half-mile, virtually every car, even the winner's, has been stamped by a black "doughnut," the evidence of a side-to-side meeting with another car. At Richmond, a sort of hybrid of big and little tracks, drivers race on an oval that is almost perfectly suited to fast but tight competition. At Bristol, the thirty-six-degree banks turn the half-mile into a land of lightning, producing some of the fiercest—and most anticipated—racing of the year.

ROAD COURSES

80

NASCAR Winston Cup Series drivers proved they also could turn right many years ago. NASCAR road racing got its start on June 13, 1954, on a winding road course pieced together from runways at the Linden, New Jersey, airport. Al Keller got the win and made another bit of NASCAR history, driving a Jaguar to victory lane to give foreign car builders their only NASCAR Winston Cup victory. Linden is long gone, but road racing lives in the NASCAR Winston Cup Series. Road-course events anchor each coast—at Sears Point Raceway, middle and opposite, in Sonoma, California, and at Watkins Glen International, top, in Watkins Glen, New York. There's even a road course in Japan that has hosted NASCAR-sanctioned races—Suzuka Circuit. The NASCAR Winston Cup Series held two exhibition events there in 1996 and 1997. Featuring tight and sweeping turns, uphill and downhill sections, and dramatic runs through series of "esses," the courses provide a different sort of challenge for drivers accustomed to thousands of miles on oval tracks. Mechanics also face an unusual hurdle, for preparing a car for road-course racing requires a new approach.

The decade of the 1960s was perhaps the most tumultuous in NASCAR history. It was a time of profound change; of new faces in victory lane; of majestic, newly built speedways, of turmoil and problem-solving. NASCAR racing grew up and out, expanding its competitor base and its constituency while changing the face of its competition with bigger tracks and faster speeds.

NASCAR Winston Cup racing's landmark event of the decade's first year occurred June 19, 1960, as the Grand National Series attempted a feat never before proposed—a six-hundred-mile race. The World 600 was scheduled May 29 at the new Charlotte Motor Speedway (now Lowe's Motor Speedway) in Concord, North Carolina, but construction difficulties and weather problems pushed the spring race date into the next month.

The process of building the track, NASCAR's third paved superspeedway, was difficult, and it stretched the bank accounts of builders Bruton Smith, an aggressive racing promoter, and Curtis Turner, an even more aggressive driver, beyond their limits. The removal of bedrock granite from the construction site elevated expenses and delayed work. Bad weather further complicated matters. And the first race week was one of the most unusual in NASCAR's storied history.

NASCAR AT THE
CROSSROADS

Jammed grandstands cheer the start of the Coca-Cola 600 in 1997 at Charlotte Motor Speedway. The track, opened in 1960 and now known as Lowe's Motor Speedway, has been a leader in growth and innovation since the 1970s.

As cars circled the 1.5-mile track in practice and qualifying runs, the new asphalt came up in chunks, leaving potholes. On the day before the race, more than eight hundred tons of fresh asphalt was placed on the surface. On the morning of the 600, two questions persisted: Could drivers and cars last six hundred miles, and would the track hold together under the relentless pounding?

Some answers came quickly, as portions of the track separated early. But mechanics were ready. Many had mounted wire screens on the fronts of their cars to protect radiators and engines from debris.

The race was filled with wild, multicar wrecks. As pieces of the track broke apart, cars left the race with broken axles and blown tires.

Jack Smith, one of NASCAR's pioneer drivers, was rolling along in a swift Pontiac in position to be the marathon's top survivor. He had a five-lap lead and had led 198 laps when a chunk of asphalt ruptured his fuel tank, spurting gasoline. Despite the best efforts of his crew to stop the flow, Smith had to leave the race. Joe Lee Johnson took over first place and reached the checkered flag first, scoring the only win of his career.

Remarkably, the day of relative chaos ended with no significant injuries. But the financial troubles associated with the track's construction eventually chased Smith and Turner from CMS. Smith would return to regain control of the speedway more than a decade later. In the interim, it was run with considerable skill by Richard Howard, a Catawba County, North Carolina, farm boy who grew up to be a successful furniture store owner and racing promoter. Howard, using innovative promotions such as paying five-figure sums to pole winners and building trust with drivers, saved CMS from financial disaster and positioned it for the Smith-led building program that later would make the track one of the best in the world.

Major tracks joined the schedule as NASCAR expanded its reach and influence into new parts of the country.

Atlanta International Raceway (now Atlanta Motor Speedway) also opened in 1960, with Fireball Roberts winning its first race. Other major tracks would join the schedule as the decade rolled on and NASCAR expanded its reach and influence into new parts of the country.

In NASCAR garages, the presence of Detroit automobile manufacturers became much more of an issue. Ford Motor Company and Chrysler Corporation fought fiercely and face-to-face through their NASCAR racers for much of the decade, with many observers figuring that sales of fleets of new automobiles and American industrial dominance hung in the balance.

Newspaper, magazine, and television advertisements were used to trumpet wins by drivers after NASCAR victories, urging consumers to rush to their car dealerships to "drive the car that won Daytona."

Detroit has been involved in NASCAR racing in some fashion—often with very big bankrolls, sometimes with sly behind-the-scenes help—virtually since the beginning. Constant one-upmanship by the factories and their designers and engineers led to bigger, better, faster, sleeker race cars as each company tried to outthink and outmaneuver the others. Among the results were monster engines, cars with big rear wings, and special performance vehicles that tested—and ultimately broke through—the boundaries of NASCAR rules.

Ever faster

The 1960s saw a new focus on superspeedway racing with the continuing growth at one of the circuit's mainstays, Darlington Raceway, along with the addition of Michigan Speedway in the southeastern part of the state. Consistently upgraded over the past thirty years, Michigan continues to be a major stop in the NASCAR Craftsman Truck Series, the NASCAR Busch Series, and the NASCAR Winston Cup Series.

Perhaps most illustrative of the war between the manufacturers were the 1960s tussles over Chrysler's supremely powerful Hemi engine and the Dodge and Plymouth winged racers, brilliantly designed and aesthetically pleasing automobiles that gave a futuristic look to NASCAR Winston Cup Series racing.

Chrysler put its 426-cubic-inch Hemi engine on the front lines of NASCAR racing in 1964. Having watched Ford dominate the previous three seasons, Chrysler's decision makers opted for a huge dose of new horsepower for the new year. The new powerplant shot speeds at Daytona International Speedway, the circuit's fastest track, to unheard-of levels with Paul Goldsmith running to the Daytona 500 pole at a speed of 174.910 mph. The best Fords hit only the high 160s. On race day, Richard Petty, driving behind Hemi power, was untouchable. Driving a potent Plymouth prepared by his cousin, crew chief Dale Inman, and his brother, engine builder Maurice (an exceptional triumvirate that would produce some of NASCAR's best seasons), Petty led 184 of the 200 laps and was out front for the final 149.

Petty won the 1964 national championship, the first of his seven titles, but Chrysler lost its big gun, the Hemi, the next season when NASCAR banned the motor. Chrysler balked, pulling out of NASCAR racing in protest. Petty detoured to drag racing, driving a Plymouth Barracuda with Hemi power. Halfway through the season, a NASCAR reversal allowed the Hemi to run at tracks of one mile or less, returning Chrysler to the fold.

With car manufacturers certain that winning on the racetrack translated to sales on the showroom floor, representatives from the car builders often clashed with NASCAR on the rules front. Occasionally there was enough disagreement to launch a manufacturer boycott. Generally, after a few months or a year or so of grumbling and trading insults, everybody made up and came back to the party.

Race car technology reached a new level late in the 1960s with the development of Chrysler's winged automobiles—the Dodge Daytona and the Plymouth Superbird. Responding to superior performance by Ford's Torino and Mercury Cyclone models, Chrysler engineers went to work to produce a car silhouette unlike any that had been seen. Their creation sent shock waves through NASCAR racing and fascinated car buyers who liked muscle machines. The Daytona and Superbird were supremely sleek, with sweeping, crisp lines and a bold "racy" look. Their most striking feature was a tall wing that rose from their rear decks. This gave the cars a sort of airplane-on-the-ground appearance, and engineers and car builders salivated at the thought of how they might look—and run—on NASCAR's biggest speedways.

Would the cars be fast? Test driver Charlie Glotzbach answered that question quickly, spinning a speed of more than 200 mph at a Chrysler testing facility. The winged racers made their competition debut on September 14, 1969, in the inaugural race at Alabama International Motor Speedway in Talladega, with Dodge Daytona driver Richard Brickhouse riding the hot new rocket to its first victory over a field decimated by a driver boycott.

The Hemi engine shot speeds at Daytona International Speedway, the circuit's fastest track, to unheard-of levels.

Red hot at Daytona

Paul Goldsmith stunned the racing world in 1964 at Daytona, gunning a Hemi-powered Plymouth to a speed of 174.910 mph. The top Fords peaked out in the high 160s.

On wings of Dodges

In the 1960s, Detroit's manufacturers began to design faster, sleeker cars like Bobby Allison's Dodge Daytona, which carried a tall wing on its rear deck.

Ford vs. Chevy vs. Pontiac

The battle between automobile manufacturers in stock car racing is as old as the sport. Detroit movers and shakers invest money, time, technology, and engineering expertise in the chase for the checkered flag, a race that often finds fans declaring allegiance to car makes with as much fervor as they do favorite drivers. Tommy Thompson won a NASCAR race at Detroit in 1951, below left, as Bill France took his road show to the heart of the automobile industry. Even in racing's early years, race cars became billboards for auto makers, as evidenced by the swath of advertising on Marshall Teague's Hudson, below opposite.

From the first race in what would become the NASCAR Winston Cup Series through the first half-century of stock car racing's top circuit, the link between the race-track and the automobile industry has been a front-burner subject.

When Kansan Jim Roper won the first NASCAR Winston Cup (then Strictly Stock) race June 19, 1949, in Charlotte, North Carolina, he drove a Lincoln. Apparent winner Glenn Dunnaway had been disqualified, giving the victory to Roper. But NASCAR officials removed the engine for technical inspection, leaving Roper in a jam. He had driven the Lincoln from Kansas to Charlotte for the race, and, with nothing under the hood, was a somewhat perplexed winner of a landmark event. How would he get home? Mecklenburg Motors of Charlotte stepped forward and gave Roper a new engine so he could hit the road. It was a small step, one of the first "deals" between the automobile industry and these new men called stock car racers.

Many, many others would follow in a sometimes-rocky marriage that has had dramatic impacts on both partners.

It was no surprise when racers and the people who built, sold, or worked on automobiles joined hands. More than a few of the early race cars carried lettering boasting of the prowess of Joe's Garage or Mack's Filling Station. Joe and Mack liked racing, after all, and they gave the car owner twenty or thirty bucks to help with the fuel and tires. Probably got them in the pits, too.

Racers and their business friends were able to bene-fit—indeed, they still are—from a loyalty people outside the sport often find curious, and that is the average Joe's attraction to a particular brand of automobile. "My Ford can beat your Chevy any day of the week," a refrain heard at practically every drive-in restaurant of the 1950s, became a real challenge on the racetracks of the period. And fans who drove Fords to the track were eager to see their Chevrolet buddies left in the dust.

The automotive industry picked up on these links and began to play a role in NASCAR racing in the early years. In 1950, driver Marshall Teague worked out a deal with the Hudson Motor Company to support his racing efforts, and Teague's race car was easily distinguished from the rest of the field by the large FABULOUS HUDSON HORNET lettering emblazoned on its sides. Teague used "heavy-duty" parts built by Hudson to strengthen his cars for the rugged dirt tracks on the NASCAR circuit. Nash later joined in to support Curtis Turner as car builders recognized the value of identi-fying themselves with the hot drivers of the day.

Bill France Sr., still strengthening the heart of his racing organization in 1951, made some key inroads with the potentates of the automobile industry as his top racing series visited Detroit to run the Motor City 250 on August 12. It was the city of Detroit's 250th anniversary, and officials

decided to celebrate with a 250-lap race on the one-mile dirt track at the Michigan State Fairgrounds. France jumped at the chance to display his racers in front of the city's auto industry hierarchy. Packard provided the pace car. The show was a wild one, and Tommy Thompson won in a Chrysler, attracting immediate and prolonged attention from Chrysler people in the pits. France left town with a better perspective on Detroit's attitude toward stock car racing, and with more than a handful of new contacts.

By 1954, Hudson was touting the attributes of its cars in publication advertisements by emphasizing the Hudson's "national championship" in racing. Similar boasting by other manufacturers would follow through the years as Detroit linked its motorsports success to the power and stability of its cars in an attempt to sell the general public on racing as a proving ground. "Win on Sunday, sell on Monday" became a popular slogan.

NASCAR tracks became competition arenas for the car manufacturers, and Detroit engineers and car designers became much more involved in the goings-on at speedways,

trying to help race teams with insider information, technical support, and "heavy-duty" or "endurance package" equipment that could bolster a car's showing. Performance on the track meant pride on the road.

As highly publicized battles between Ford, Chrysler, and General Motors heated up, teams and manufacturers began to build special cars and look for every advantage within (and sometimes outside) the rules. The result, on occasion, was a tug-of-war between NASCAR and the manufacturers, as NASCAR tried to write its rules so that competition would be equal and the cars "stock," while Detroit car builders sought every advantage for their particular model sometimes developing exotic engines and "space-age" car designs. NASCAR occasionally intervened to end such adventures, declaring a certain type of engine ineligible or preventing a particular model from competing. The car manufacturers sometimes balked, sparking periodic boycotts when these disagreements occured.

Detroit put millions of dollars into stock car racing, each manufacturer supporting its top teams (they had so-called "factory rides") with financial help and mechanical advice. The 1960s were the high point of the "factory days," with each car builder flooding NASCAR racing with engineering assistance and public relations gusto. In the ebb and flow of competition, one make would show gains over the previous season, often encouraging drivers to jump ship and go with

"the other guy." The factories tried to recruit and keep the best and the brightest and were forever on the lookout for upcoming talent or proven drivers on other circuits.

In NASCAR Winston Cup's modern era, there have been the "Big Three": Chevrolet, Ford, and Pontiac. Each manufacturer takes a different approach to its racing than it did thirty years ago, but the competition between these factories to win has not changed. Each has support personnel as well as engineering and technology departments that contribute to their at-track performance. In fact, in 1999, Dodge announced it would return to the "stock car wars" in 2001, competing in NASCAR Winston Cup for the first time in two decades.

The manufacturers also have used NASCAR racing to benefit assembly-line production of passenger cars. A 2.5-mile asphalt track on a hot Sunday afternoon with forty-three cars racing within inches of each other at 200 mph is a good proving ground for ideas and equipment, and manufacturers are able to use race results in transferring technology to passenger automobiles. Detroit also places its engineers in the racing environment as members of NASCAR Winston Cup teams, not only putting them where they can help the teams but also giving them a chance to discover ways racing can help build better street vehicles.

Detroit and Daytona continue to work together, their cars and drivers now racing with the finest equipment and the best knowledge.

The blistering speed of the winged cars concerned NASCAR officials. In August 1970, NASCAR announced that each eligible NASCAR Winston Cup Series car would be required to use a carburetor restrictor plate, a device designed to limit fuel and air flow to the carburetor, thus choking speed. The plate trimmed speeds at Talladega by more than 10 mph and quickly became a valuable—if controversial—device in NASCAR's battle against accelerating speeds.

The plate rule was a hard punch for Chrysler to absorb. Then the final blow for the winged cars came in 1971 when NASCAR announced that certain cars, including the Daytona and Superbird, would be limited to engines of 305 cubic inches for that season. That penalty effectively spelled the end of the winged racers.

> Through the 1950s and into the next decade, Roberts helped carry racing from its dirt-track origins into the new superspeedway age of the 1960s.

A pair of stone walkways leads to the crypt in a quiet corner of Bellevue Memorial Gardens in Daytona Beach. Off in the distance, on a race day, the thunder of cars can be heard at Daytona International Speedway.

Here lies Edward Glenn "Fireball" Roberts, the man many call stock car racing's first significant star. The marker on his crypt, accented with checkered flags and a bust of Roberts, lists his racing accomplishments and offers visitors the message that he "brought to stock car racing a freshness, distinction, a championship quality that surpassed the rewards collected by the checkered flag."

Born in 1929 in Tavares, Florida, and introduced to racing in the late 1940s by his Daytona Beach buddy Marshall Teague, Roberts brought a new flair to a growing sport. He won in only his third NASCAR Winston Cup Series appearance August 13, 1950, at the tough Occoneechee Speedway in Hillsboro, North Carolina. Through the 1950s and into the next decade, Roberts helped

carry racing from its dirt-track origins into the new superspeedway age of the 1960s. Smart and a thinking man's driver ("He could map out a camshaft in no time flat," said mechanic Ray Fox), Roberts studied mechanical engineering for more than three years at the University of Florida before moving on to race full time.

Roberts, whose greatest fame came while behind the wheel of No. 22 Pontiacs fielded by Smokey Yunick, had won thirty-two NASCAR Winston Cup Series races and was riding along in the upper reaches of the sport in 1964 when he sustained fatal injuries in an accident at Charlotte Motor Speedway.

The wreck happened on the eighth lap of the World 600. Junior Johnson and Ned Jarrett touched coming off the second turn, sending Jarrett into the inside wall and Johnson spinning through the middle of the track. Roberts, trying to avoid the accident, spun into the inside wall, hit an abutment, and flipped. The impact ruptured the fuel tank in Roberts's car, and the damaged vehicle began to burn. Jarrett ran over to help him get out of the car.

Roberts was treated at Charlotte Memorial Hospital (now Carolinas Regional Medical Center), which added telephone lines to deal with the flood of calls about his condition. On July 2, weakened by pneumonia and a blood infection, Roberts died. He was only thirty-five. Writing in *The Charlotte News* that day, Max Muhleman penned a memorable opening to one of the first stories about the death of a great

A man, a mountain

Fireball Roberts won thirty-two times on NASCAR's top circuit and blazed a trail of excellence and style that others would seek to follow. He is considered by many to be stock car racing's first superstar. Opposite: Roberts (No. 22) fights Buck Baker (No. 300-C) for the inside line at Raleigh Speedway in 1956.

racer: "Fireball Roberts, perhaps the most nearly perfect of all stock car drivers, is dead and it is like awaking to find a mountain suddenly gone."

Muhleman, who covered motorsports and was among Roberts's circle of friends, left sportswriting not long after the driver's death. Muhleman said Roberts was unique in his approach both to racing and to life.

"He was maybe the first guy to become a big winner by using brains and discipline as well as bravery and skill levels," Muhleman said. "I think of Curtis Turner, in particular, as being an archetype of the old sort of drivers who came up on dirt tracks. Fireball did, too, but he recognized that, as asphalt tracks came on board, the technique was different, and he adapted to it in a very thoughtful and calculated way. He was the first driver I was aware of who worked out with weights, and he was interested in things other than racing. You could talk to him about religion and politics, about things other than racing and girls."

Over the stretch of a year, from January 1964 to January 1965, stock car drivers Joe Weatherly, Billy Wade, Jimmy Pardue, and Roberts died from injuries sustained in on-track accidents. In the 1964 Indianapolis 500, a crash claimed the lives of Eddie Sachs and Dave MacDonald. "It was hard to think about racing again," Roberts had said of the death of the popular Weatherly, one of the hard chargers and grand pranksters from the sport's early years. Weatherly, Curtis Turner's wisecracking sidekick and a superb driver in his own right (he was Grand National champion in 1962 and '63), was killed January 19, 1964, when his car hit the wall in the sixth turn of the Riverside, California, road course. Only a few months later, Roberts, too, was dead, and concern about safety became pervasive. "I would say that most drivers felt that something needed to be changed as far as improvement for the safety of the drivers,'" said Ned Jarrett. "There was concern."

Officials and manufacturers responded. The evolution of the stock car from showroom automobile to purpose-built racer has been a complicated one, marked first by rudimentary adjustments by shade-tree mechanics and,

> **"Most drivers felt that something needed to be changed for the safety of the drivers."**
> — DRIVER NED JARRETT

in the modern era, by seemingly minor but profound aerodynamic changes suggested by high-tech tools of the computer age.

Safety concerns prompted many of the technological advances. Roll bars, used to strengthen the roof and sides of cars, were added in the early 1950s after wrecks frequently resulted in cars flipping onto their roofs. Although roll cage assemblies now are strong and state of the art, early designs were less than scientific. David Pearson, for example, once used one of his mother's old metal bed frames to fashion roll bars.

Drivers' seats have evolved from the front-seat "bench" style used in many passenger cars to factory-installed bucket seats to individually designed, custom-fitted bucket-type seats molded for each driver's body. Seat belts and shoulder harnesses keeping drivers in their seats also have advanced dramatically from the early days, when many drivers used no belt at all and some used makeshift restraints made of cord or pants-style belts.

Extra protection

After a series of crashes, car builder and team owner Cotton Owens (left) devised a roll-bar system that added an elbow-high bar for increased safety. Driver David Pearson gives the new system a look.

JOE WEATHERLY

Evolution in safety

Until the 1960s, safety technology like Ralph Earnhardt's lap belt, above, had been only somewhat effective. Left: Darlington Raceway president Bob Colvin (left) and driver David Pearson examine a fuel cell developed by Firestone in 1964. The rubber cell dramatically improved safety conditions by reducing the risk of fire.

NASCAR Safety: Rapid Response

In the 1960s, NASCAR made gains in safety equipment and procedures. NASCAR pit roads have been staffed by officials and fire department personnel, below and top right, who are trained to respond quickly when fire or threat of fire exists. Gasmen on NASCAR pit crews, opposite, wear helmets and other protective items to guard against injury. Inner tire liners, second from top right, have helped prevent disastrous blowouts. Among other advances through the years was the development of magnaflux testing, second from bottom right, to uncover potentially dangerous cracks, invisible to the naked eye, in metal parts that are then rejected, bottom right.

Safety first

Roll cages, roof flaps, and sturdy car construction usually prevent injuries even in huge wrecks like this one in the 1999 Daytona 500.

Some drivers in NASCAR's early years balked at the idea of items like seat belts and harnesses designed to hold them in their seats. They wanted freedom of movement inside the cars, and they were concerned about being trapped in their seats if a wreck resulted in fire.

The most significant changes related to safety probably have been in fire protection and tire stability. Racers typically used regular street tires in NASCAR events before the development of special racing tires late in the 1950s. In 1966, the creation of the inner liner, a so-called "tire within a tire," dramatically lowered the possibility of major accidents caused by blowouts. That process evolved into today's large racing radials, which were introduced to NASCAR competition in April 1989 at North Wilkesboro, North Carolina. By 1993, the bias-ply tire was history in the NASCAR Winston Cup Series.

For many years, fire was the driver's biggest worry. Race cars moving at high speeds and carrying large quantities of gasoline were potential infernos waiting to be ignited. In 1965, Firestone developed a protected rubber fuel cell to fit inside the gas tank. Fire-related problems declined significantly. Fire-retardant driving suits (early racers drove in T-shirts and jeans) also protected drivers from injury.

Additional refinements throughout the years have added to driver safety. Helmet design advanced from the football-type helmets of the late 1940s to the exotic full-face helmets worn today. Mesh window netting was developed to keep drivers completely within their cars during accidents. In 1993, after high-speed spins resulted in numerous cars going airborne, NASCAR developed roof flaps, rectangular insets in car roofs that open when a car spins backward, creating an air brake that keeps the car on the ground. In 1999, officials added wheel restraints to cars to prevent wheels from separating from vehicles during accidents.

Not all advancements have been safety-related. In the early 1980s, power steering was introduced to NASCAR Winston Cup Series racing, sparking a minor revolution within the sport and making handling of monster stock cars significantly easier for drivers. NASCAR's pioneer drivers tell stories of huge race cars like the Hudson Hornet and the Oldsmobile 88 and the strength needed to handle them on old washboard dirt tracks. It wasn't unusual in those days for a driver to hop out of a car after a race with hands that were bruised and sore from struggling with the steering wheel for two hundred laps. Although new chassis designs and innovations by talented mechanics helped to smooth rides, the arrival of power steering was one of the giant steps in making drivers more comfortable through long, competitive races.

Many of the foundational changes in car building and preparation occurred in the mid-1960s as NASCAR moved from racing cars sold in dealership showrooms to built-for-racing vehicles. Mechanic Ralph Moody was the first to develop a standard ready-made chassis for racing, moving the sport a quantum leap from the "strictly stock" chassis configurations of the previous seasons. That opened the door for individuals like Banjo Matthews, a former driver and top mechanic, to start businesses that supplied fully prepared cars for racers. Matthews's Arden, North Carolina, shop led that field for years. Mike Laughlin and Ronnie Hopkins now are top guns in the speed-for-sale business, and several leading teams construct their own cars from the ground up, totally within the confines of their shops.

"In the fifties, the cars were pretty stock," said Ned Jarrett. "We had just the basic roll bar coming over the driver's head. In the early sixties we started adding more roll bars and eventually got to the concept of the roll cage that is much like the design we have today. The sixties also was the time when we started making special chassis parts as opposed to welding to strengthen what was already

> Many changes in car building occurred in the mid-1960s as NASCAR moved from racing cars sold in dealership showrooms to built-for-racing vehicles.

Reinventing the tire

In the 1960s, Goodyear engineers developed the tire inner liner to provide an added level of protection when tires blow. Late in the 1980s, the company introduced radial tires to NASCAR racing.

there. Before, it was a matter of just welding a piece of metal onto the car's A-frame to make it more durable. But people started making special, stronger A-frames for racing and special spindles that were larger and stronger."

Another major addition to race-day technology was the two-way radio, a way of communicating between race car and pit that quickly became one of the most important safety devices in NASCAR history. Spotters located at high vantage points around racetracks could immediately warn drivers of wrecks. Driver-pit communication elimi-nated the need for pit boards, large signs used by pit personnel to alert drivers to key information during a race. Although the first crude use of a two-way radio in a NASCAR race occurred in 1952, widespread use of more sophisticated devices came about in the mid-1970s.

Engineering and technological advances in auto racing led to the transfer of ideas to passenger-car development. Manufactur-ers' strong ties to motorsports led to stronger bodies for passenger cars, advances in steering and chassis mechanisms, and better passenger-car tires, among other things. Racing became the perfect testing ground for new ideas and innovations, for five hundred miles of pounding on asphalt provided the ultimate inquiry into substance and strength.

Changes in technology and the increasingly tough nature of NASCAR racing threw a spotlight on a part of stock car competi-tion that has been a component of the sport since the begin-ning—pushing the envelope on rules. From the first NASCAR

> **NASCAR's inspectors have lowered the boom on drivers and mechanics who were "just interpreting the rule book."**

Winston Cup Series race, when apparent winner Glenn Dunn-away was disqualified for using "bootlegger" springs on his car, innovative mechanics have sought ways to circumvent rules in search of the extra edge that can be the difference between first and second place.

Sometimes, their chicanery succeeds. On many other occa-sions, it fails, as evidenced by the bounty of illegal parts NASCAR inspectors have confiscated over the years. Among the hundreds of items: a brick, added to a car to meet weight requirements but painted to resemble a two-way radio; a hydraulic device designed to lower a car's rear deck; tires soaked in chemicals to improve grip; gas cans modified to force a faster fuel flow.

Discovery of such illegal items has prompted a variety of reactions from NASCAR officials over the years. From huge fines to probation and suspensions, NASCAR's inspectors have low-ered the boom on drivers and mechanics who were, in the words of the late, great crew chief Harry Hyde, "just interpreting the rule book."

While on-track speeds shot up through much of the 1960s, NASCAR Winston Cup Series teams also were learning to boost their victory chances by refining the art of the pit stop. In racing's early years, the act of driving a car onto pit road for tires and fuel was often a painfully slow process. Tires were changed with standard lug wrenches, and gasoline often was splashed into tanks with little regard for speed. Crew chiefs soon learned, however, that precious seconds saved in the pits translated to hundreds of yards gained on the racetrack. Teams began experimenting with pit stops that were much better orchestrated and with individual pit assignments for team members who specialized in tire changing, tire carrying, fueling, or wielding the heavy jack used to boost the car for tire work.

Just checking

NASCAR developed body templates such as the one used by David Pearson, opposite, in 1967 to check car bodies for proper design. Occasionally, mechanics "over engineer" their cars, resulting in confiscation of illegal parts, at left on display near the NASCAR mobile office.

THE INSPECTION: HIGH AND LOW

Every car entered in a NASCAR Winston Cup Series race undergoes a detailed inspection prior to competition. Pinpoint devices and officials verify that each car has the proper ground clearance, top, and roof height, bottom. The inspection station, staffed by officials who travel from race to race, is a busy spot prior to qualifying and in the hours before a race as car after car, fine-tuned by mechanics, passes under the scrutiny of inspectors trained to catch infractions. Each car must meet minimum clearances in a number of areas, and templates are used to check conformity to standard body designs. A minor variation in the way a car body is shaped or its height can make a major difference on the race track. Similar inspection procedures are used in the NASCAR Busch Series and NASCAR Craftsman Truck Series in an attempt to keep competition close and the playing field level.

Fit for a race

Officials use an assortment of metal templates,
above and left, to confirm that each car meets
NASCAR specifications at all angles.

The Wood brothers—a team led by Glen and Leonard Wood from Stuart, Virginia, and filled out by their assorted relatives and friends—are given the most credit for bringing rapid speed and ballet-like precision to pit stops. With the arrival of air wrenches to speed tire changes, the Woods turned the pit stop into a science in the 1960s. Their ability to methodically change four tires and refuel their cars in the twenty-second range set a standard for other teams and opened the door for faster and faster stops that pushed into the sixteen-second vicinity.

The Woods's pit-road skills quickly became big news across the landscape of American motorsports, earning them an invitation to participate in the Indianapolis 500 in 1965. Ford Motor Company, aware of the Woods's prowess in NASCAR circles, arranged for them to pit Jim Clark's Lotus-Ford in the 500. Although the Woods had never worked with an Indy-car, they studied one of the team's backup cars, figured out ways to make fuel flow more rapidly and handle tire changes more quickly, and waited confidently for the race. No tire changes were needed because of Clark's smooth driving, but his fuel stops wound up in the eighteen- to twenty-second range, much faster than typical Indy-car stops. He won the race and gave much of the credit to the Woods's slick pit work.

NASCAR Winston Cup Series pit stops evolved over the years as equipment changed and team members began physical workout programs to gain strength and agility. In the 1990s, some top teams designed their crew operations so that their more athletic members worked almost exclusively on pit stops, using their speed and practiced movement patterns to trim more and more fractions of seconds from pit stop times. The result often was the difference between first place and second.

As the 1960s drew to a close, advances in technology, both as it related to race cars and racetracks, were changing the world of NASCAR dramatically. The old was giving way to a new day. During the 1970 season, NASCAR Winston Cup Series reached the end

Pit stop evolution

Joe Littlejohn talks to driver Curtis Turner, top, while Frank Christian puts fuel in Turner's Oldsmobile during a race in the early 1950s. The Wood Brothers team of Stuart, Virginia, above, made pit stops seem routine and became the kings of pit road while working with driver David Pearson. Modern-day NASCAR Winston Cup crews rush to change tires and add gas, opposite, during a pit stop sequence at Las Vegas Motor Speedway in 1999.

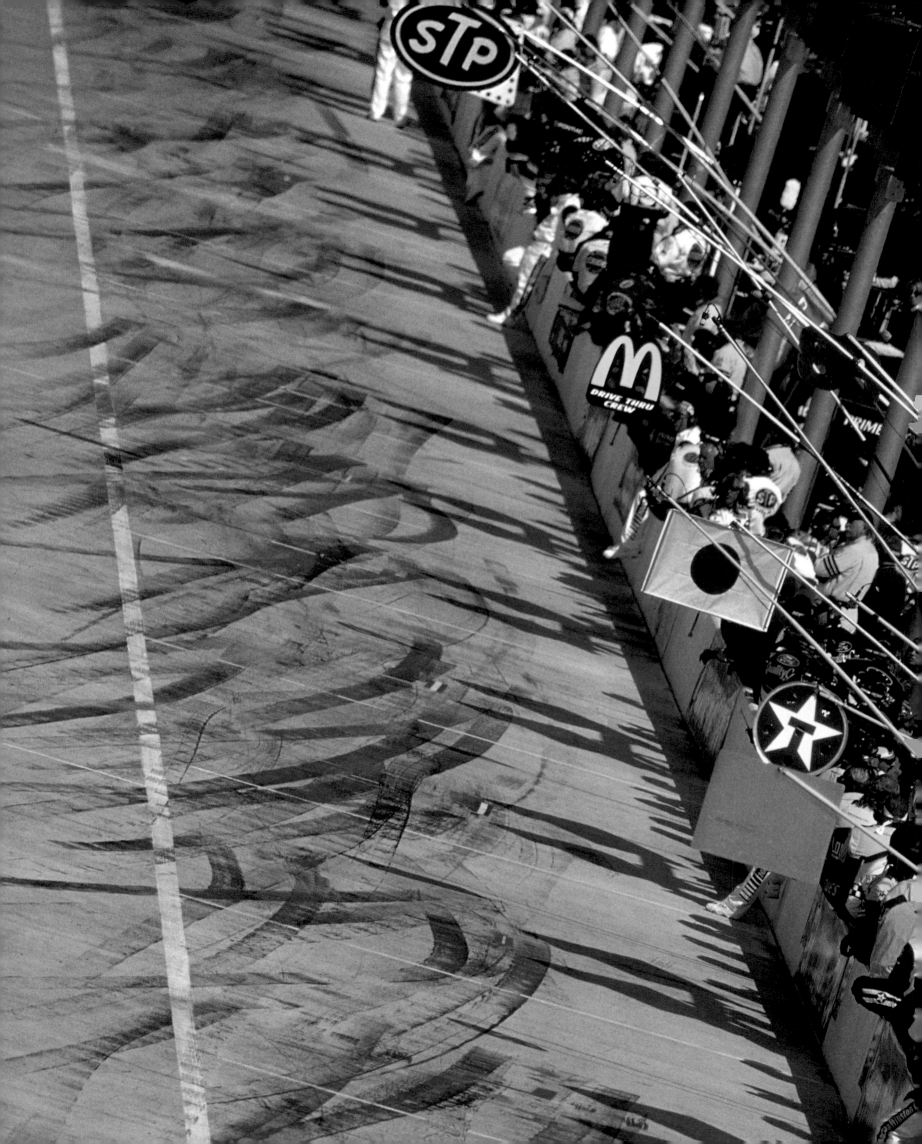

of one road, running its final dirt-track race. Perhaps fittingly, Richard Petty, the man who had ruled much of the decade, was the winner in the Home State 200, the Series' last run on dirt, at the half-mile State Fairgrounds Speedway in Raleigh, North Carolina, on September 30.

Earlier that year, on the Alabama International Motor Speedway course, Buddy Baker took the sport light years from the dirt, running a practice lap at 200.447 mph in a Dodge Daytona, marking the first official time a stock car had broken the 200 mph barrier on a closed course.

The decade ended with Richard Petty and David Pearson having established their dominance and drivers like Jim Paschal, Dick Hutcherson, Marvin Panch, and Paul Goldsmith having shown that they, too, could score repeatedly at stock car racing's highest level. The field they raced on was constantly moving through the '60s as speed, technology, and equipment changed markedly. Rewards increased, too. Money-won totals soared into six figures, but none of the drivers had any inkling of the big numbers waiting around the corner.

Quick change

A suddenly silent pit road, opposite, shows the tire marks left by departing racers after a round of pit stops. NASCAR Winston Cup teams have become experts at speedy engine changes, above, usually replacing powerplants in ten to fifteen minutes.

As NASCAR moved into its "middle years" at full throttle, it watched the 1960s end and the '70s begin with the promise of a grand new dimension of racing. With a firm foundation established, the sport's leaders worked toward putting a finer focus on the daring drivers who were taking stock car racing to new levels.

For much of its first twenty years, NASCAR had been largely defined by its machines—first the juiced-up jalopies of the late 1940s, then the boxy family sedans of the '50s, and super muscle cars of the '60s. Now the spotlight focused on the drivers behind the steering wheels of these powerful rides, men (and occasionally women) who would add color, drama, and a fierce competitive spirit to NASCAR racing as it grew to become an ever-bigger force in the world of American spectator sports.

Part of the new vista for the sport had been created in the northern Alabama foothills by Bill France Sr. As the 1960s neared an end, Alabama International Motor Speedway, a 2.66-mile track located between Birmingham and Atlanta, opened as Daytona's sister facility. France wanted his second speedway to be a little longer—and a little faster—than Daytona. The track, later renamed Talladega Superspeedway, opened with the first running of the Talladega 500 on September 14, 1969. That race weekend in Alabama developed into one of the most turbulent in NASCAR history.

THE CREATION OF
SUPERSTARS

Opposite: David Pearson (left) and Richard Petty, the sport's giants in the 1960s and 1970s, check out the sights of New York City. Another driver who garnered substantial media attention was Janet Guthrie (second from right), who was part of the Ring Free 10L All-Girl Racing Team, above.

Construction of the Talladega facility began in May 1968, and, even in the early months, it became evident that the track would be physically imposing. Its banking measured thirty-three degrees, and the long backstretch and sweeping front tri-oval obviously would be speed alleys. This racecourse would produce some fast laps.

Too fast, it turned out. Early tests on the track indicated that tires were blistering under the 195-mph-plus speeds registered by drivers. Rumors spread quickly through the racing fraternity, and teams arrived at the speedway for Talladega 500 week with many questions.

In qualifying, Charlie Glotzbach drove a winged Dodge Daytona to a world closed-course record speed of 199.466 mph, sending shock waves through the garage. The track was too rough and the tires too brittle for such speeds, drivers said.

On Friday of race weekend, special tests by drivers Donnie Allison and Glotzbach resulted in more tire problems. Firestone, then chasing Goodyear in NASCAR competition, withdrew from the race. On Saturday morning, the Professional Drivers Association (PDA), a group drivers had formed earlier in the year to pursue retirement, pension, and insurance plans for drivers and to improve conditions at the tracks (Richard Petty was president), met and decided not to race in the 500 because of safety concerns.

On Saturday, the track hosted a race for NASCAR Grand Touring division cars. The GT series began in 1968 and allowed in its eligibility rules compact and "sports"-type cars, including the Ford Falcon and Mustang, Mercury Cougar, Pontiac Firebird, and Chevrolet Camaro. From 1968 to 1973, cars that fit into the category raced in several similar NASCAR divisions, including Grand American and Grand National East. The Saturday Talladega race for the GT

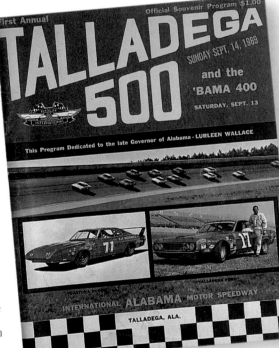

cars was held without serious incident, and France declared that Sunday's race would be run as scheduled. The PDA requested that the race be postponed until the tire companies could produce tires more suited for the high-speed surface, but France refused. He ran laps on Saturday in a Holman-Moody Ford, testing the track himself.

After much discussion, thirty drivers, including most of the day's stars, left the track on Saturday, towing their cars behind them. France insisted that the race would be held, suggesting that drivers should run only as fast as their equipment allowed. On race day, the field consisted of thirteen NASCAR Grand National cars and a fill-in group of NASCAR Grand Touring automobiles from the previous day's event. The crowd of almost fifty thousand attending Talladega's first race was told that ticket stubs from the event could be exchanged for a ticket to any future race at Daytona or Talladega.

The race proceeded without a major problem, although seven cautions slowed the pace. Drivers ran slower laps than those that had been recorded in qualifying and practice runs earlier in the week. Richard Brickhouse, a relatively unknown driver from Rocky Point, North Carolina, whose odds to win would have been astronomical before the driver walkout, rode Ray Nichols's Dodge Daytona to victory lane, beating Jim Vandiver by seven seconds.

It was an awkward birth, but NASCAR's fastest speedway was on its way. Soon it would be hosting some of the most dramatic finishes in racing history. And the best drivers in the world would be back to participate in them.

> NASCAR's fastest speedway was on its way. Soon it would be hosting some of the most dramatic finishes in racing history.

Rush hour

Traffic at NASCAR's biggest superspeedways routinely produces three- and four-wide racing.

NASCAR's ever-expanding pool of driving talent gave the sport some of its most competitive days. Richard Petty settled into his reign as King, but David Pearson, a smart, calculating driver from South Carolina, challenged him. Petty and Pearson became the giants of the period and symbols of the new group of superstars as NASCAR Winston Cup Series racing claimed a bigger part of the American sports consciousness. The role of the driver was changing. Just as Mickey Mantle had exemplified the Yankees and John Havlicek the Celtics, Petty, Pearson, and the top guns that followed became the out-front faces of their sport, men who would speed NASCAR to new heights of popularity.

As attention began to focus on the remarkable runs of success NASCAR's stars were stringing together, an important changing of the guard occurred at the top level of the sport.

The drive, ambition, tenacity, and persistence of Bill France Sr. had given NASCAR its foundation. France was founder, president, rules maker, promoter, salesman, garage-area lawyer, and much more. "He was King Kong," said Ray Fox Sr., longtime NASCAR mechanic–car owner and, later, a NASCAR inspector. In other words, France carried the big stick. He was Big Bill.

Many could not envision NASCAR without Senior at the helm. The sanctioning body had been so much his baby, molded to the framework he wanted and the parameters he allowed. Yet France, whose wife, Anne B., also worked in NASCAR and Daytona speedway offices, had a plan for seamless family management of the organization upon his retirement. Sons Bill Jr. and Jim had been groomed on the testing grounds—at race sites—to learn the France way of doing things.

Their time arrived at a key point in NASCAR history. The organization was moving from big to bigger, shedding the rougher edges of its past and racing toward a richer future. The year 1972

would represent the dividing line between those two eras, and the precise day that brought the change was January 10, when Senior handed Junior the keys to the kingdom. William Henry Getty France retired as NASCAR president, and William Clifton France—not technically a junior but called so for convenience sake so often that the moniker stuck—stepped up.

Junior had been educated for this role from his teenage years. He sold snow cones in the Darlington Raceway infield at the first Southern 500 in 1950. He sold programs on the old Daytona Beach-Road course. He hammered advertising posters onto telephone poles. He parked cars. "We worked the motorcycle races together at Daytona [on the beach course] in 1949," said Jim Bockoven, a friend of France's and a classmate at Seabreeze High School in Daytona Beach. "He did everything. He put bumper strips around telephone poles. He worked hard. He had a perfect kind of attitude for this business."

Petty, Pearson, and the top guns that followed became the out-front faces of their sport, men who would speed NASCAR to new heights of popularity.

A checkered for Mario

Mario Andretti, driving a Holman-Moody Ford (No. 11) to victory lane, won the 1967 Daytona 500. It was the only NASCAR Winston Cup Series victory for Andretti, opposite, one of the great race car drivers of all time. Andretti and other leading open-wheel drivers detoured to NASCAR racing on occasion, and some stayed permanently, infusing the NASCAR Winston Cup circuit with new talent.

Presidential decree

NASCAR president Bill France Jr., addressing the seasonal awards banquet in New York City in 1998, took the reigns from his father at a time when focus was shifting to drivers.

He even raced cars. In the mid-1950s, France drove in competition here and there, mostly at Carolina and Virginia short tracks. After two years at the University of Florida and a stint in the Navy, France returned to Daytona Beach to take on bigger roles with his father's guidance. He worked on both the NASCAR side of the hall and inside Daytona International Speedway offices. During construction of the speedway, he was very involved in hands-on work, often operating a large, rolling compactor to pack the surface as the track took shape. He became an important player as larger tracks expanded the nature of the sport in the '60s and was being prepared for the presidency as the '70s beckoned.

On April 4, 1966, NASCAR lost one of the key executives from its formative years. Pat Purcell, who became NASCAR's executive manager in 1952 and executive vice president in 1964 and made many of the day-to-day business decisions in those years, died in Ormond Beach, Florida. Bill France Sr. called him "a sturdy rudder in rough seas, a tower of strength when the burden was heavy." There would be many others in the Purcell mold over the years—individuals who contributed greatly to the advancement of the NASCAR style of auto racing and established the foundation upon which great growth occurred but whose labors weren't necessarily seen by the general public. Men like Joe Epton, Bill Tuthill, Ed Otto, Houston Lawing, Jim Foster, and Morris Metcalfe gave NASCAR a strong foundation for its years of expansion.

Although Junior inherited this impressive base of executive support and his father remained an active participant in NASCAR operations, the ship became his to steer in 1972. Those looking for a weak spot, a place where they could take advantage of this changing of the guard, had trouble. Junior could be as tough as Senior if the circumstances called for such posturing.

"I'm probably more conservative than he was," Junior said. "My mother was very conservative. From a business risk standpoint, I take a little longer to sort through everything. I try to be pragmatic. If he liked the idea, he jumped. And he landed a lot more than he didn't. He had a pretty good knack from a vision standpoint of seeing what's around the curve. He could forecast that pretty good."

Junior is particularly skilled in management and has the ability to see the big picture in all circumstances. He can cut through layers of fluff to get to the heart of an issue quickly, and his ability to run one of sports' largest organizations has attracted attention from corporate leaders and other entertainment and sports executives around the world.

Former NASCAR officials remember the working lunches that Junior hosted in the NASCAR dining area, where he occasionally fixed grilled cheese sandwiches loaded with butter for everybody. NASCAR executive Les Richter would bring in some tamales and somebody else a jar of peanut butter, and there they would sit, planning the future of one of the country's fastest growing sports organizations while dining on quick and easy cuisine.

ISC leader

Jim France, the younger son of "Big Bill," has taken a more behind-the-scenes role throughout his tenure at NASCAR. In 1987, he became the president and chief operating officer of International Speedway Corporation.

Jim France, Senior's younger son, also was involved in NASCAR and speedway operations at a young age and through the years has been a constant adviser to first his father and now his brother. Jim usually works in the background, but keen observers of the goings-on in Daytona know him to be one of the most talented individuals and progressive idea people in the business. Since 1987, he has been president and chief operating officer of International Speedway Corporation (ISC), the multifaceted Daytona Beach-based motorsports company that owns speedways at Daytona Beach, Talladega, Darlington, and numerous other locations. ISC also operates such racing entities as the Daytona USA tourist attraction and MRN (Motor Racing Network), which broadcasts many NASCAR events. Jim France also serves as executive vice president and secretary of NASCAR. As sidelights, he has raced motorcycles, Legends cars, and Allison Legacy cars. "What Jim brings to the table is a practical but often fresh approach to the situation," said one NASCAR insider. "He has a great mind, and he's very pragmatic like Bill. He's not comfortable in the limelight."

Anne B. France, who worked in finances and ticket operations in Daytona until 1991, died in January 1992. Bill Sr., who had been stricken with Alzheimer's disease eight years earlier, died in June of the same year.

As Bill France Jr. stepped into the biggest of offices in Daytona, NASCAR was beginning to enjoy a new age of growth, both in recognition and finance. Now Richard Petty, David Pearson, and those chasing them had much more money and prestige to pursue. The pioneer drivers of the past, men like Tim Flock, Buck Baker, and Lee Petty, looked at the new, big numbers in wonder as the groundwork was being laid for Dale Earnhardt, Mark Martin, Darrell Waltrip, and Jeff Gordon, the superstars of future years.

> **As Bill France Jr. stepped into the biggest of offices in Daytona, NASCAR was beginning to enjoy a new age of growth.**

Petty steadily built on his legend. Handsome, popular with fans, and embraced by the news media, he was a new sort of race car driver. Realizing early that signing autographs, answering reporters' questions, and generally putting a pleasant face on racing would produce large dividends, Petty became his sport's goodwill ambassador in an era when the sport was ripe for growth and outreach. He took a penmanship course to improve his handwriting, the result being a distinctive, flowing signature now owned by countless legions of racing fans. His fan base grew like weeds on the roadside. "Petty for President" bumper stickers popped up. Soon, he became known as King Richard. Petty would be the most important figure as NASCAR racing grew from a regional peculiarity to an international phenomenon. Some say the graph of NASCAR's success and its climb from backwoods to boardrooms can be charted on his strong back.

Petty solidified his stature in 1967, enjoying a season that, barring some sort of superhuman, cosmic effort, never will be duplicated.

Presidents and kings

Richard Petty, above and opposite, drove to twenty-seven victories in 1967 in a blue No. 43 Plymouth and was featured on a NASCAR record album, left.

"I'VE NEVER BEEN SCARED IN A RACE CAR"
RICHARD PETTY
and The Roaring Sound of NASCAR
in STEREO

Legendary drivers (from left) Tiny Lund (in plaid shirt), Bobby Allison, Mario Andretti, and Dick Hutcherson shoot the breeze while waiting for the 1967 Daytona 500 drivers' meeting to begin. Clyde Lynn is in foreground.

David Pearson, a master at superspeedway racing and a winner six times at Daytona International Speedway, celebrates in victory lane after a successful Firecracker 400 run.

In a striking blue Plymouth with a white No. 43 on the side, Petty rode into motorsports history, enjoying the sort of dominance that few athletes reach across the spectrum of competitive sports. Although the times were different (the schedule was much longer, fields were sometimes uneven in strength, and eleven of Petty's victories were in races of one hundred miles or less), the accomplishments of the Petty team that season cannot be diminished.

Petty won an astounding twenty-seven times, a figure roughly equivalent to an NFL team going unbeaten or a baseball team finishing ten games in front of second place. Within that total, though, is an even more remarkable statistic: Petty won ten straight races. In NASCAR's modern era, no one has been able to win more than four in a row.

Pearson, the driver who would be Petty's nemesis for much of his career, learned to race on the dirt tracks of the Carolinas. He got his big break in the second World 600 in May 1961 at Charlotte Motor Speedway, accepting an invitation to drive a Pontiac for Ray Fox Sr. The 600 belonged to Pearson. He won the race despite wrestling with a flat tire over the final two laps. Victories at Atlanta and Daytona followed, and Pearson began building his reputation as a big-track master. "He just had a natural instinct about what to do," Fox said.

Pearson had raced his own cars in twenty-two NASCAR Winston Cup Series events in 1960 and had done well enough to be named series rookie of the year. But the connection with Fox and the unlikely victory at Charlotte launched his career. Over the next twenty-seven years, he would be linked with some of the best teams and mechanics in the sport, and he would ride into legend in an eight-year run with the Wood brothers team, dominating superspeedways, winning poles simply as a matter of course, and displaying some of the best strategic driving ever seen. Seldom a run-and-gun, foot-to-the-floorboard racer, Pearson often won by lurking, preserving the strength of his equipment until late in a race, and then challenging for the win.

> **Pearson often won by lurking, preserving the strength of his equipment until late in a race, and then challenging for the win.**

It worked 105 times, giving him the second-biggest victory total in the sport's history and carrying him to national championships in 1966, '68, and '69. When the sport began to hit its stride in the 1970s, he was ready to show the full power of the art he had perfected on the tiny bullrings of the Carolinas.

Pearson began to flex his muscles in the sport at about the same time as Junior Johnson was moving from one level to another, giving up a successful driving career to become a team owner and provide top-notch machinery for some of the stars of the next era. Few individuals touched as many parts of NASCAR's first half-century as Robert Glenn Johnson Jr.

Johnson rode the dirt and asphalt of the 1950s and '60s to dozens of NASCAR Winston Cup Series victories, displaying a rough-and-ready driving style that emphasized a heavy right foot and little patience. He retired from driving in 1966 but had only begun to make an impact on racing. For the next thirty years, he enjoyed stunning success with an impressive list of drivers that included Darrell Waltrip, Cale Yarborough, Neil Bonnett, and Terry Labonte. Johnson's Ingles Hollow, North Carolina, shop

From driving to directing

After retiring from racing in 1966, Junior Johnson made a seamless transition to car owner, continuing his winning ways until his retirement in 1995.

became a training ground for some of the best engine builders and mechanics in motorsports.

Johnson left the sport in 1995, selling his Junior Johnson and Associates racing team and moving to a new home near his old Wilkes County, North Carolina, stomping grounds. He ended his NASCAR career with 50 on-track wins, 139 victories as a car owner, NASCAR Winston Cup Series championships with Waltrip and Yarborough, and a legacy as one of the shrewdest operators in motorsports. He was usually a step ahead of trends, a season ahead of his competitors in evaluating driving talent, and, often, a lap in front of the field.

Johnson's impact stretches far beyond his exploits within the confines of the racing oval, however. He became something of an American icon, the perfect representation of the good ol' boy racer from the southern backwoods, the whiskey runner turned Daytona champion.

Or, in the considerable judgment of noted American author Tom Wolfe, Johnson is "the last American hero." In an article in *Esquire* magazine in 1965, Wolfe, who would become one of America's most widely known journalists and novelists, told the story of stock car racing through the life and times of Johnson. Johnson had stepped out of the North Carolina mountains, a plain man with a poor background, to become a new American legend of sorts.

Wolfe followed Johnson on the NASCAR circuit for much of a year, popping in at selected races and roaming the Wilkes County countryside that was Johnson's home. "He would show up, work on it, and leave," Johnson said. "I wouldn't help him because I wanted him to do his own story the way he saw it instead of me trying to influence him and tell him the good side of everything and leave out the bad. One of the things that has always stuck with me is that when he first called me he said he had just finished doing a story on Liz Taylor. I said, 'Why in the world do you want to talk to me if you just left Liz Taylor?'"

> **Although he became known as Gentleman Ned, Jarrett didn't hesitate to trade fender paint when necessary.**

Among those who raced side by side with Johnson was Wendell Scott, the most successful African American driver in NASCAR history and the only one to score a victory in the NASCAR Winston Cup Series. In that race, held December 1, 1963 (but counted as part of the 1964 season), in Jacksonville, Florida, Scott, one of only six African American drivers in NASCAR Winston Cup history, crossed the finish line first but didn't officially get the victory until hours later. His win, accomplished despite the constant financial struggles the Virginia driver faced, was not the celebrated occasion it should have been. Officials originally awarded the win and the trophy to Buck Baker. Scott was declared the winner after a recheck of scorecards, but the decision came too late for him to enjoy the spoils of victory lane and the accolades traditionally heaped on the first-place finisher.

A difficult road

Wendell Scott (right), with driver Charlie Scott (no relation), raced in the NASCAR Winston Cup Series for thirteen years, winning a race at Jacksonville, Florida, in December 1963 to score the only victory by an African American driver in the series' history.

Two-time champion

Ned Jarrett, known as Gentleman Ned, racked up two NASCAR Winston Cup Series championships in the 1960s before retiring to pursue a career in broadcasting.

Fearless

Fred Lorenzen, handsome and charming, was a fan favorite
throughout his brief but flashy career.

Scott, a resident of Danville, Virginia, rode against the wind in stock car racing for thirteen years, overcoming racism that was indicative of that era. He retired from driving in 1973 with twenty career top-ten finishes.

Joining Johnson in retirement in the 1966 season was Ned Jarrett, who had started racing in 1953 and recorded two national championships (1961 and '65) and fifty race wins during a steady, splendid career. Although he became known as Gentleman Ned, Jarrett didn't hesitate to trade fender paint when necessary, and he did so with some of the best drivers of NASCAR's formative years.

Stepping into the places of drivers like Johnson and Jarrett were men like Fred Lorenzen, whose success earned him two memorable nicknames—Golden Boy and Fearless Freddy.

An Illinois short-track star with film-star features and a crop of blond hair, Lorenzen rolled south early in the 1960s in an attempt to transfer his United States Auto Club (USAC) stock car success to NASCAR. He won twenty-six NASCAR Grand National races in a career that ended far too soon.

Lorenzen won the USAC stock car championship in 1958 and '59 and was drawn to the headlines being written about Daytona, Darlington, and the good ol' boys of the NASCAR circuit. Although he had run seventeen races in two previous seasons, Lorenzen got his big NASCAR Grand National break when Ralph Moody invited him to join the potent Holman-Moody Ford team in 1961. It was a proposal Lorenzen didn't have to hear twice. He teamed with some of the best mechanics in Ford racing history and won three times in 1961. He became one of the flashiest superspeedway drivers of all time and, in 1963, became the first NASCAR driver to win $100,000 in a season.

The most remarkable thing about Lorenzen's career, however, may be its brevity. Deciding he had won enough money and bothered by stomach ulcers, Lorenzen retired from driving in 1967 at the age of thirty-two. Drivers now race into their fifties. Lorenzen later regretted the decision and tried comebacks in 1970, '71, and '72 but never enjoyed the success of the early 1960s.

Another comet streaking across those years was that of LeeRoy Yarbrough, a naturally talented driver who won the first race he ever entered as a sixteen-year-old at Jacksonville (Florida) Speedway. Yarbrough raced on the NASCAR Grand National tour for the first time in 1960 and won a few races through the middle years of the decade before hooking up with car owner Junior Johnson to startle the circuit with seven superspeedway victories and $200,000 in winnings in 1969. He won the Daytona 500, the World 600, and the Southern 500 that season and swept every major national driver-of-the-year award. Everywhere that racers gathered, Yarbrough's run through the tour's major races was the talk of the town.

Sadly, his stay at the top was very short. Over the next two years, he was involved in several accidents, including one in practice for the Indianapolis 500, and he steadily declined. He left racing late in 1972.

> Everywhere that racers gathered, Yarbrough's run through the tour's major races was the talk of the town.

A national superstar

LeeRoy Yarbrough was the talk of the 1969 season as he won seven superspeedway races and swept every major driver-of-the-year award.

Richard Petty charged into the 1970s with style, winning twenty-one times in 1971, eight in '72, six in '73, and a total of twenty-three in '74 and '75. He won five of his record seven NASCAR Winston Cup Series championships in the 1970s.

A master on both tiny bullrings and the huge Daytona tri-oval in the 1960s, Petty underlined his superstar status with continuing high performance in the 1970s, leading the way as NASCAR's increasing popularity generated a long line of extraordinary drivers. As NASCAR's attendance numbers grew, fans came to watch Pearson, Cale Yarborough, Bobby Allison, Darrell Waltrip, Buddy Baker, and Benny Parsons battle the King for supremacy.

The 1971 and '72 seasons were as different as night and day for NASCAR. The '71 season was the final year of the "long" schedule, one that typically carried drivers, teams, and officials to far-flung speedways scattered all over the country and sent them into battle two and three times a week.

The arrival of the R.J. Reynolds Tobacco Company (RJR) as the series' primary sponsor in 1971 served as a jumpstart to discussions to trim the schedule. "We wanted to work on really building the series up," Bill France Jr. said. "It's difficult to do that with fifty races and trying to get all the drivers there. We started off with 250 miles as a minimum distance." That meant an end to the two-hundred-lap, hundred-mile races on half-mile tracks that had been a staple of NASCAR schedules virtually since the beginning. When RJR tacked its Winston name on the series in 1971, only those races of 250 miles or more in length were considered part of "NASCAR Winston Cup Series" competition, although points earned in all races counted toward the seasonal championship. In 1972, the

> The big eye of television was starting to look at NASCAR racing much more favorably, impacting the sport in many compelling ways.

shorter races were removed entirely, and the schedule was cut to thirty-one events. Thus began what later would be labeled as the "modern era" of NASCAR racing.

The NASCAR Winston Cup Grand National series immediately gained more importance as a chain of more or less equal events as opposed to an unruly hodge-podge of short and long races scattered across a map. Winning the NASCAR Winston Cup Series championship thus became a more significant line on a driver's resume—not to mention the extra money that RJR brought to the table.

Racing suddenly became a more profitable enterprise for many. Although Detroit factories had frowned on dumping piles of money into the sport, RJR was bringing cash in by the truckloads, big-buck sponsors were signing on, and—of momentous importance—the big eye of television was starting to look at NASCAR racing much more favorably. That fact ultimately would impact the sport in many compelling ways.

For most of NASCAR's first twenty years, television saw NASCAR (and motorsports in general) as a difficult child. The races were too long for television broadcasts. The audience was perceived to be regional. And, besides, who would watch five hours of cars going around and around and around in circles?

Before television became a close partner with NASCAR in its astonishing growth of the 1980s and '90s, the big cameras approached the sport gingerly. There would be many small steps before the first big one. But, slowly, NASCAR's drivers learned about this new way to spread their story and made it a major player in the growth of NASCAR.

The first live network television production of NASCAR Winston Cup Series racing occurred when CBS Sports broadcast two twenty-five-mile qualifying races for the Daytona 500, along with a pair of compact car races, all contested at Daytona International Speedway. The next year, ABC Sports televised portions of the

Up close, personal

Television showed a new side of racing's personalities. ABC's Chris Economaki interviews A. J. Foyt, left.

Firecracker 250 at Daytona. It became standard practice for the networks to either join races in progress—updating viewers on any significant activities that had transpired before the broadcast, or to tape them and show them at a later date.

ABC showed portions of the 1962 Daytona 500, and reporter Chris Economaki, a now-legendary print and broadcast journalist, was working pit road. "The ABC crews were all union," Economaki remembered. "A lot of them were older guys. When there came an assignment in Florida in the middle of winter, they all wanted it. So I had a lot of old guys down there with me, including my cable puller [although TV equipment is very portable now, in the early 1960s crews had quite a task moving cameras and other gear]. The race started, and Fireball Roberts came off the corner and into the pits after about ten laps, which, of course, was surprising. I said to the guy, 'Let's go!' He said, 'There's a car coming.' I said, 'I know, that's why we're going.' "

Economaki, who has been present at many NASCAR high points, also was a key player in the first live green-flag-to-checkered-flag television broadcast of a NASCAR Winston Cup Series race. That historic event occurred April 10, 1971, when ABC broadcast the Greenville 200 from the half-mile Greenville-Pickens Speedway in upstate South Carolina. The network used its ninety-minute anthology program, *ABC's Wide World of Sports*, to showcase the NASCAR Winston Cup Series.

Illustrating television's concerns about going live with NASCAR racing was the elaborate planning, discussion, and unorthodox policy that surrounded the Greenville-Pickens event. "About a month before the race, a guy from ABC in New York called," said Pete Blackwell, then and now the track's operator. "They had talked to Bill France, and they were looking for a race they could get in on *Wide World of Sports* in an hour and a half. They had gone through results sheets and saw that we had finished a race in about an hour and twenty-five minutes. So the guy asked me if I thought we could do

that again. I said, 'Sure,' although there was no way I could be sure."

The race broadcast had to fit in the ninety-minute television window for *Wide World of Sports*. NASCAR officials, eager to help ABC, trimmed the starting field for the race from thirty cars to twenty-six, the idea being that fewer cars on the track should mean fewer caution flags and, thus, a faster race.

"I remember telling Richard Petty before the race that this could lead to bigger things," Blackwell said. "I said, 'Please, no cautions.' He said, 'You won't have to worry about cautions. I'm going to lead all the way. Just tell everybody to follow me.' "

Scaffolding had been erected at spots around the track for ABC's cameras, and a portable studio was set up near the first turn to house announcers Jim McKay and Economaki. A technician handling the feed from the track to New York had to be headquartered in one of the track's rest rooms.

"We were kind of worried about the crowd," Blackwell said. "I felt like everybody might stay at home because it was on TV. But it worked the other way around. Everybody wanted to be here to see it." The grandstands were full hours before the start of the race.

In-car camera

Television cameras mounted inside race cars (and in other strategic locations on the cars) revolutionized the broadcast coverage of NASCAR, giving fans a "driver's eye" view of racing. Modern cameras, above, are much smaller than the one that rode with Cale Yarborough, left, in the 1980s.

The field was circling the flat half-mile on the parade lap when *Wide World of Sports* opened. After receiving a signal from a technician that the broadcast had started, flagman Bill Blackwell unfurled the green flag.

Although track, television, and NASCAR officials were more than a little nervous, the event went well. There was only one caution, and Bobby Isaac zoomed under the checkered flag first to finish the race in one hour and sixteen minutes, well within ABC's prescribed time period. The purse, boosted by television money, was $20,000, a record for a NASCAR hundred-miler.

"During the race, I got a call from a guy who said he was in a bar in Kentucky," Blackwell said. "He was watching the race and said he had made a bet with another guy about who was going to win. He wanted to know who was going to win because he was sure the race had been recorded."

Five years later, ABC had its cameras trackside at a key moment, this time showing the country the powerful drama that unfolded in the final lap of the 1976 Daytona 500, which produced what many observers rank as the best finish in NASCAR history.

Negotiations between race officials and ABC had produced an agreement that would have ABC broadcast the closing portion of the 500 live. When ABC joined the race, the chase for the win, as it did so often in those days, was coming down to Petty and Pearson, the big guns of the era. Then at the peak of their careers, they raced each other week after week across the country, their cars often (sixty-three times, in fact) finishing one-two in the tense theater of racing's final laps. Here they stood at the high point of the NASCAR Winston Cup season, in the nation's bicentennial year,

in two of the best race cars they would ever drive, and once again the decision would be theirs alone.

After the pretenders had fallen by the way-side, Petty took the race lead with thirteen laps to go. A few minutes earlier, Dennis Lewin, an ABC coordinating producer, had been talking to Roone Arledge, a producer at the ABC headquarters site in Innsbruck, Austria, where the winter Olympics were in full swing. ABC planned to switch from Daytona Beach to Innsbruck as soon as the race ended, and Arledge was checking with Lewin in ABC's New York City studios to see if things were progressing smoothly at the race location.

"He asked me if we were going to run over into the Olympics' time," Lewin remembered. "I told him, no, that everything was fine. Everything was going along as expected. Then—wham!—so much for that."

The 500 had reached its final lap. As tension mounted and ABC fired the images across the country, Pearson planted his Mercury on the bumper of Petty's first-place Dodge. As they roared down the long Daytona backstretch, Pearson accelerated and passed Petty as they entered the third turn. Pearson's momentum carried him high in the turn, and Petty dropped low, planting his car beside Pearson's as they roared into the tricky turn four with the checkered flag and a $50,000 payday in sight.

In the heart of the turn, their cars touched, the impact sending both almost head-on into the outside wall. Pearson's car bounced to the inside, hitting Joe Frasson's car near the entrance to pit road. Petty whirled out of control, spinning on the grass separating the racing surface from pit road. For an instant, their cars rested on the grass, mangled remnants of the shiny racers that had started the 500 more than three hours earlier. Then, suddenly, Pearson's car started moving, chugging slowly

Showdown at Daytona

David Pearson, opposite, reached the Daytona 500 victory lane in 1976 after a heart-pounding last-lap confrontation with Richard Petty resulted in one of the most memorable finishes in the sport's history, left.

through the grass. Calling on his years of experience and one of the quickest minds in the sport, Pearson had pressed his clutch as the wreck developed, keeping the engine running. As Petty watched in frustration while his panicked crew tried to push his car (it wouldn't start because the fan had been jammed into the radiator and wouldn't turn), Pearson moved past the No. 43 onto the asphalt and rolled under the checkered flag at about 20 mph.

It was a fabulous, heart-stopping finish. The suspense and drama had given a new color to NASCAR Winston Cup racing, and ABC was there to spread it live across the country. The Olympics had to wait. "We stayed with the race and ran over several minutes into the Olympics' time," Lewin said.

The 1976 Daytona 500 finish, besides putting another sensational layer on the Pearson-Petty rivalry, gave NASCAR one more convincing argument in an offensive designed to score additional television time for its events. "That finish was just another chip to throw out on the table that had a role in moving the sport along," Bill France Jr. said. "It was one of the better finishes."

The next of those "better finishes" came along three years later.

After extensive negotiations, France sold CBS on a racing package that included the first flag-to-flag telecast of a major NASCAR race—the 1979 Daytona 500. When the deal was finalized, France treated CBS executive Neal Pilson to lunch at the Steak 'n' Shake, a favorite France fast food restaurant at the corner of Nova Road and Highway 92 in Daytona Beach. Of course, they had no idea of the events they were setting in motion.

The morning of February 18, 1979, the Sunday of the Daytona 500, dawned to much of the eastern part of the United States in the grip of a massive winter storm. Ten inches of snow fell in South Carolina, four inches closed the Atlanta airport, and four of the five Great Lakes were frozen for the first time in modern history. The Midwest and the Northeast were being battered by a prolonged freeze, with temperatures in New York City plunging to zero. Some cities along the East Coast had five-foot snowdrifts. This was all bad news for many people, but it was a big positive for CBS and NASCAR. With impassable roads and brutal temperatures forcing millions of people inside, CBS had a much bigger potential viewing audience for its first shot at start-to-finish NASCAR coverage. And it wasn't snowing on the east coast of Florida (although the start of the race was delayed by rain).

The impact of the day's events wouldn't fully hit home until the days and weeks that followed. In fact, despite years of work leading to the television agreement, the people in the NASCAR and speedway offices in Daytona Beach approached the day with some nervous moments. "We were scared to death that it was going to hurt the crowd [attendance]," Bill France Jr. said. "We originally had probably the biggest blackout plan in the history of sports, something like seven southeastern states [where the race would not be shown on television]. But we relaxed the blackout as we got closer to the race. Finally, we left Florida in it for a while, then just dropped the blackout, period."

Smashing

David Pearson (No. 21), who finished his career with 105 NASCAR Winston Cup Series victories, usually was an expert at avoiding altercations such as this one.

The speedway was packed with more than one hundred thousand spectators, and CBS cameras beamed the start of the race across the country to begin what would become an extremely important TV sports broadcast.

After three hours of jousting on the high banks, the race came down to the final lap. Two veteran drivers, Donnie Allison and Cale Yarborough, ran one-two as the white flag fell, with Richard Petty, Darrell Waltrip, and A. J. Foyt about a half-lap behind in a battle for third. Petty, Waltrip, and Foyt were out of the running for the win—or so it seemed. As Allison and Yarborough roared down the backstretch for the last time, Yarborough moved to the inside and alongside Allison's rear quarter-panel. Allison turned left, attempting to force Yarborough low onto the track apron. But Yarborough refused to move over, and the cars banged together once, then twice. As they entered the third turn, the cars hit again, then sailed into the outside wall. As they lost power, they slid down onto the infield grass, the race—for them—over.

As CBS cameras searched the track for the new leader, Petty, who hadn't won a race in eighteen months, suddenly saw a gift opening. He rolled through the final turns and held off Waltrip at the finish to win the 500 for the sixth time. Meanwhile, at the site of the Allison-Yarborough crash, a tempest was boiling, spiced by the fact that the same three drivers—brothers Donnie and Bobby Allison and Yarborough—had wrecked earlier in the race. Bobby had stopped at the final-lap wreck scene to check on his brother. Bobby and Yarborough wound up in an argument and then a fight, and Donnie and several safety workers in the area separated them.

It was mayhem, and CBS cameras were there.

"I started around Donnie, and Donnie pulled out and carried me down into the grass," Yarborough said later. "My car started spinning, and then we both started spinning. I had the race won. There are no ifs, ands, or buts about it. And he knew it, too. It's the worst thing I've ever seen in my life in racing.

"When Bobby stopped, I went over and asked him why he did what he did. He bowed up, and I swung at him."

> "When Bobby stopped, I went over and asked him why he did what he did. He bowed up, and I swung at him."
> —DRIVER CALE YARBOROUGH

Yarborough said Bobby slowed on the final lap to act as a blocking agent for his brother. Bobby denied the charge.

Donnie, whose career would end without a Daytona 500 victory, said, "I made up my mind to go low in the third turn. He [Yarborough] was going low regardless. He wasn't going to give, and I wasn't going to give."

About an hour later, Petty appeared in the Daytona press box for the winner's interview and jokingly asked, "Where's the fight?"

CBS had scored, and scored big.

The race was the top-rated program during each half-hour that afternoon. All around the country, talk in office break rooms, at barbershops, and along Main Street was about The Fight. *Newsweek* magazine had a story and photo on the incident. The fracas, watched by many thousands of people who had never experienced a NASCAR race, drew new fans to the sport. Ticket sales for the next race on the schedule, at North

Best foot forward

Bobby Allison and Cale Yarborough wrestle after a last-lap crash eliminated Yarborough and Donnie Allison (top left corner) from the 1979 Daytona 500.

It is difficult to walk through a NASCAR Winston Cup Series garage area and not run into somebody's brother, cousin, father, father-in-law, or uncle. And all of them will be part of the show.

In NASCAR, family values have been around since the beginning. The sport of auto racing seems to naturally attract relatives of people already involved, thus expanding the family-tree aspect of the sport to dozens of intertwined branches and making any NASCAR Winston Cup garage perhaps the biggest family reunion in professional sports.

The most famous family of competitors is the one named Petty. The patriarch, Lee, got the ball rolling in NASCAR's very first Strictly Stock race in 1949. Richard followed a decade later and became the series' most prolific winner, giving the family a total of ten NASCAR Winston Cup titles. Kyle, Richard's son, began his driving career in 1979 and added victories to the family total. Adam, son of Kyle, now drives on the NASCAR Busch Series, Grand National Division and is looking at the NASCAR Winston Cup Series, spreading the Pettys' influence to a fourth generation. Richard's brother, Maurice, was the engine builder, and his cousin, Dale Inman, was the crew chief for most of his two hundred wins.

The Bakers put three generations—Buck, Buddy, and Randy—on the track. Buck and Buddy drove to hall of fame careers and Randy, Buddy's son, raced in fourteen events in the 1980s and '90s. Buddy remains in the sport as a television commentator, and Buck directs a driving school for racers.

The Allisons recorded some of the greatest highs in racing history. Bobby won eighty-four times and realized his goal of winning the NASCAR Winston Cup championship. Davey, Bobby's son, won nineteen NASCAR Winston Cup Series races and finished second to his father in the 1988 Daytona 500. Clifford, Bobby's younger son, drove in the NASCAR Busch Series. Donnie, Bobby's brother, raced from 1966 to 1988, winning ten times.

The Flock brothers—and a sister, Ethel—were stock car racing pioneers. All three brothers—Tim, Fonty, and Bob—raced in the rough-and-tumble early years of the 1940s and '50s, and all earned spots in the National Motorsports Press Association Hall of Fame. Tim was the family kingpin, winning thirty-nine times. Ethel raced in two NASCAR events in 1949.

Ralph Earnhardt started the Earnhardt family racing saga in the 1950s, and his son, Dale, arrived in 1975 and eventually became the dominant driver in NASCAR Winston Cup Series racing, winning seven championships. Dale Jr. won two NASCAR Busch Series championships before becoming a third-generation Earnhardt in the NASCAR Winston Cup Series, while son Kerry is a part-time competitor in the NASCAR Busch Series. Earnhardt's daughter Kelley is an executive at Action Performance Companies, a manufacturer of licensed products and apparel.

Three-time NASCAR Winston Cup champion David Pearson brought his sons, Larry, Ricky, and Eddie, into racing.

Relatively speaking

Brothers Terry and Bobby Labonte, above, enjoyed success in NASCAR Winston Cup's modern era; the Flock brothers (left to right), Bob, Tim, and Fonty, were hard chargers in the pioneer years.

The speedway was packed with more than one hundred thousand spectators, and CBS cameras beamed the start of the race across the country to begin what would become an extremely important TV sports broadcast.

After three hours of jousting on the high banks, the race came down to the final lap. Two veteran drivers, Donnie Allison and Cale Yarborough, ran one-two as the white flag fell, with Richard Petty, Darrell Waltrip, and A. J. Foyt about a half-lap behind in a battle for third. Petty, Waltrip, and Foyt were out of the running for the win—or so it seemed. As Allison and Yarborough roared down the backstretch for the last time, Yarborough moved to the inside and alongside Allison's rear quarter-panel. Allison turned left, attempting to force Yarborough low onto the track apron. But Yarborough refused to move over, and the cars banged together once, then twice. As they entered the third turn, the cars hit again, then sailed into the outside wall. As they lost power, they slid down onto the infield grass, the race—for them—over.

As CBS cameras searched the track for the new leader, Petty, who hadn't won a race in eighteen months, suddenly saw a gift opening. He rolled through the final turns and held off Waltrip at the finish to win the 500 for the sixth time. Meanwhile, at the site of the Allison-Yarborough crash, a tempest was boiling, spiced by the fact that the same three drivers—brothers Donnie and Bobby Allison and Yarborough—had wrecked earlier in the race. Bobby had stopped at the final-lap wreck scene to check on his brother. Bobby and Yarborough wound up in an argument and then a fight, and Donnie and several safety workers in the area separated them.

It was mayhem, and CBS cameras were there.

"I started around Donnie, and Donnie pulled out and carried me down into the grass," Yarborough said later. "My car started spinning, and then we both started spinning. I had the race won. There are no ifs, ands, or buts about it. And he knew it, too. It's the worst thing I've ever seen in my life in racing.

"When Bobby stopped, I went over and asked him why he did what he did. He bowed up, and I swung at him."

> "When Bobby stopped, I went over and asked him why he did what he did. He bowed up, and I swung at him."
>
> —DRIVER CALE YARBOROUGH

Yarborough said Bobby slowed on the final lap to act as a blocking agent for his brother. Bobby denied the charge.

Donnie, whose career would end without a Daytona 500 victory, said, "I made up my mind to go low in the third turn. He [Yarborough] was going low regardless. He wasn't going to give, and I wasn't going to give."

About an hour later, Petty appeared in the Daytona press box for the winner's interview and jokingly asked, "Where's the fight?"

CBS had scored, and scored big. The race was the top-rated program during each half-hour that afternoon. All around the country, talk in office break rooms, at barbershops, and along Main Street was about The Fight. *Newsweek* magazine had a story and photo on the incident. The fracas, watched by many thousands of people who had never experienced a NASCAR race, drew new fans to the sport. Ticket sales for the next race on the schedule, at North

Best foot forward

Bobby Allison and Cale Yarborough wrestle after a last-lap crash eliminated Yarborough and Donnie Allison (top left corner) from the 1979 Daytona 500.

Carolina Motor Speedway in Rockingham, suddenly boomed. In retrospect, the day was one of the biggest in NASCAR history, and many observers say the NASCAR growth spurt that reached stunning proportions in the late 1980s and '90s actually began in the third turn that February in Daytona.

Among the drivers riding the new wave of NASCAR success in the 1970s was Benny Parsons, who won the 1973 NASCAR Winston Cup Series championship in unlikely fashion. After riding through a year of consistently good finishes and little trouble, Parsons entered the final race of the season in October at Rockingham with a substantial point lead over Richard Petty. Parsons needed only a decent finish to lock up the championship, which would be a major coup for his underfinanced team. Only thirteen laps into the long race, he met trouble, hitting Johnny Barnes's spinning car. With his ride heavily damaged, Parsons limped into the pits, almost certain that his day of glory and year of triumph had disappeared in one unfortunate accident.

But crew chief Travis Carter and his team jumped on the repairs immediately, and crewmen from other teams, all hoping to help one of the "little guys" succeed, came to assist. Parsons's rebuilt car returned to the track and stayed in the race long enough to seal the championship.

Less than two years later, Parsons would reach the peak of his career, fulfilling a dream by winning the Daytona 500. All along pit road, rival crewmen stepped forward to congratulate Parsons, now a popular racing television announcer, as he drove to victory lane—striking evidence of the respect in which he was held.

Many of the speedways that hosted the NASCAR Winston Cup Series expanded seating and refurbished facilities during the growing years of the 1970s. Perhaps key among them was Charlotte Motor Speedway. Richard Howard ran the track until 1975, boosting attendance with such ploys as paying Junior Johnson to build a

competitive Chevrolet (a brand that had been absent from the highest levels of racing for years) for Charlotte competition. Bruton Smith, who had built a huge financial empire with a string of automobile dealerships after leaving CMS, returned to Charlotte in 1975 to continue the job he had started in 1959. Smith acquired enough CMS stock during his absence to eventually regain control of the facility late in 1975. He hired former Firestone field representative H. A. "Humpy" Wheeler to run the facility and, over the next fifteen years, they turned the track into a motorsports showplace. Smith took all sorts of gambles, building condominiums at the track (people laughed, but the idea was a success) and later lighting the facility for night racing (people said it wouldn't work; it was an immediate hit, a move that led to lights at other large tracks).

With Smith and Wheeler, an enterprising promoter who has spiced Charlotte events with all manner of unusual sideshows, at the helm, their new entity, Speedway Motorsports Inc., went to the New York Stock Exchange as a publicly traded company in 1995. Soon there was a Big Three in track ownership circles: International Speedway Corporation; Penske Motorsports, started by motorsports entrepreneur Roger Penske; and Speedway Motorsports. In 1999, Penske merged with ISC, forging an alliance that dominated NASCAR Winston Cup Series racing and stretched ISC's reach from coast to coast. The ISC family grew again in December 1999 with the announcement that the corporation had purchased Richmond International Raceway (RIR) in Virginia for $215 million. RIR had been operated by NASCAR pioneer Paul Sawyer and members of his family since the 1950s.

Bonanza for Benny

Benny Parsons, now a popular television announcer, enjoyed a very successful driving career, capped by his win in the Daytona 500 in 1975.

Still, even with the giants operating big groups of tracks, there was room for "independents." Bob Bahre built a track in Loudon, New Hampshire, and soon began hosting sellout crowds at NASCAR Winston Cup Series events. In the Pocono Mountains of eastern Pennsylvania, owner Joe Mattioli welcomed NASCAR Winston Cup Series racing to Pocono Raceway in 1974, and the triangular track has been a strong part of the schedule since. Clay Earles, who opened Martinsville speedway before NASCAR was formed, continued to oversee expansion and improvement of his track—along with grandson and track president Clay Campbell—virtually until his death in 1999.

All provided great playing fields for the new generation of racers. Daytona International Speedway, however, continued to be respected as the cathedral of stock car racing because of its size, its history, and its ability to produce both remarkable speeds and tight, often breathtaking racing.

Although the track's configuration—a near-perfect tri-oval course with double doglegs in the front and a long, straight backstretch—has not been changed since its 1959 opening, racing at Daytona has been impacted significantly by the arrival of the carburetor restrictor plate. Prior to the plate's appearance, races at Daytona and Talladega, its sister high-speed track, often were decided by the infamous slingshot, a passing method that involved drafting along behind a car as closely as possible, then taking advantage of the vacuum effect caused by the draft to pull out and be propelled around that car. When the latest version of the plates appeared after Bobby Allison crashed into the frontstretch fence at Talladega in 1987, cars were robbed of substantial momentum, and the slingshot move effectively became dormant.

The 1975 season saw the debut of a new championship point system, one that remains in use today. Devised by longtime stock car racing statistical guru and public relations expert Bob Latford (who started work on the system with doodles on a cocktail napkin in a Daytona Beach bar), it eliminated the confusing framework of the old formula, rewarded consistently high finishes, and penalized failure to complete races. Drivers receive points at each finish position in a NASCAR Winston Cup Series race. The winner receives 175 points, second place 170, third place 165, and so on, with the point differential decreasing at lower levels of the finish order. Additionally, every driver who leads a lap receives five

bonus points, and the driver who leads the most laps receives an additional five bonus points.

While NASCAR's Winston Cup Series was perfecting its format, other series that still exist today were popping up, widening NASCAR's burgeoning audience. The Touring Series includes the Goody's Dash and the RE/MAX Challenge, formerly the ARTGO Challenge, which both got their starts in 1975 and have brought regional racing to new levels. The Goody's Dash Series features "scaled-down" NASCAR Winston Cup–type cars and puts drivers in subcompact racers on both short tracks and superspeedways. Cars typically raced in the series are the Pontiac Sunfire and Grand-Am, the Ford Probe, and the Chevrolet Cavalier. The series is concentrated in the Southeast, with most races scheduled in the Carolinas. Several NASCAR Winston Cup drivers ran Goody's Dash cars before they moved up. The RE/MAX Challenge Series is NASCAR's newest Touring Division, having scheduled competition for two seasons. Races are held on a variety of tracks, including Pikes Peak International Raceway in Colorado, Rockford Speedway in Illinois, I-70 Speedway in Missouri, and Gateway International Raceway near St. Louis.

Dueling at Daytona

David Pearson (No. 21) edges Richard Petty in one of their classic July finishes at Daytona.

It is difficult to walk through a NASCAR Winston Cup Series garage area and not run into somebody's brother, cousin, father, father-in-law, or uncle. And all of them will be part of the show.

In NASCAR, family values have been around since the beginning. The sport of auto racing seems to naturally attract relatives of people already involved, thus expanding the family-tree aspect of the sport to dozens of intertwined branches and making any NASCAR Winston Cup garage perhaps the biggest family reunion in professional sports.

The most famous family of competitors is the one named Petty. The patriarch, Lee, got the ball rolling in NASCAR's very first Strictly Stock race in 1949. Richard followed a decade later and became the series' most prolific winner, giving the family a total of ten NASCAR Winston Cup titles. Kyle, Richard's son, began his driving career in 1979 and added victories to the family total. Adam, son of Kyle, now drives on the NASCAR Busch Series, Grand National

Division and is looking at the NASCAR Winston Cup Series, spreading the Pettys' influence to a fourth generation. Richard's brother, Maurice, was the engine builder, and his cousin, Dale Inman, was the crew chief for most of his two hundred wins.

The Bakers put three generations—Buck, Buddy, and Randy—on the track. Buck and Buddy drove to hall of fame careers and Randy, Buddy's son, raced in fourteen events in the 1980s and '90s. Buddy remains in the sport as a television commentator, and Buck directs a driving school for racers.

The Allisons recorded some of the greatest highs in racing history. Bobby won eighty-four times and realized his goal of winning the NASCAR Winston Cup championship. Davey, Bobby's son, won nineteen NASCAR Winston Cup Series races and finished second to his father in the 1988 Daytona 500. Clifford, Bobby's younger son, drove in the NASCAR Busch Series. Donnie, Bobby's brother, raced from 1966 to 1988, winning ten times.

The Flock brothers—and a sister, Ethel—were stock car racing pioneers. All three brothers—Tim, Fonty, and Bob—raced in the rough-and-tumble early years of the 1940s and '50s, and all earned spots in the National Motorsports Press Association Hall of Fame. Tim was the family kingpin, winning thirty-nine times. Ethel raced in two NASCAR events in 1949.

Ralph Earnhardt started the Earnhardt family racing saga in the 1950s, and his son, Dale, arrived in 1975 and eventually became the dominant driver in NASCAR Winston Cup Series racing, winning seven championships. Dale Jr. won two NASCAR Busch Series championships before becoming a third-generation Earnhardt in the NASCAR Winston Cup Series, while son Kerry is a part-time competitor in the NASCAR Busch Series. Earnhardt's daughter Kelley is an executive at Action Performance Companies, a manufacturer of licensed products and apparel.

Three-time NASCAR Winston Cup champion David Pearson brought his sons, Larry, Ricky, and Eddie, into racing.

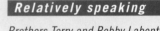

Relatively speaking

Brothers Terry and Bobby Labonte, above, enjoyed success in NASCAR Winston Cup's modern era; the Flock brothers (left to right), Bob, Tim, and Fonty, were hard chargers in the pioneer years.

Larry has raced in the NASCAR Winston Cup Series and NASCAR Busch Series, Ricky is a leading crew chief, and Eddie has worked for several teams.

Ned and Dale Jarrett are one of the most popular father-son combinations in racing. Ned retired as a driver in 1966 and moved into work as a television commentator for racing broadcasts, putting him in position to "call" Dale's run to the Daytona 500 checkered flag in 1993. Glenn, another Jarrett son, had a brief driving career before also moving into television work. Patti, Ned's daughter, is married to Jimmy Makar, crew chief for Joe Gibbs Racing and former crew chief for Dale Jarrett, his brother-in-law.

Sterling Marlin followed his father, Clifton "Coo Coo" Marlin, into NASCAR Winston Cup racing and scored the family's first victory in the 1994 Daytona 500.

The Bodines, from Chemung, New York, brought a northeastern flavor to NASCAR Winston Cup Series racing in the 1970s. Geoff, the oldest brother of the trio, began his NASCAR Winston Cup career in 1979.

Brett followed seven years later, and Todd, "Baby Bodine," arrived on the scene in 1992. All are still involved in NASCAR racing.

Several other collections of brothers currently race on NASCAR tracks—Ward and Jeff Burton; Terry and Bobby Labonte; Darrell and Michael Waltrip; David, Jeff, and Mark Green; and Rusty, Kenny, and Mike Wallace. Along the way, there have been others—Benny and Phil Parsons, Dick and Ron Hutcherson, Ron and Ken Bouchard, Billy and Bobby Myers (Bobby's son, Danny "Chocolate" Myers, is a crewman for Richard Childress Racing), Herb and Donald Thomas, LeeRoy and Eldon Yarbrough, and Jimmy and Speedy Thompson.

Other father-son driver combinations include Jabe and Ronnie Thomas, and Marvin and Richie Panch.

The Wood brothers team dynasty is in its second generation, with brothers Eddie and Len and their sister Kim, now running the show for their father Glen and his brother Leonard. Master mechanic Buddy Parrott paved the way for two sons, Todd and Brad, to join the circle of top pit players in the sport.

Much of driver Bill Elliott's success has come with the help of brothers Ernie (a crew chief and engine builder) and Dan (a transmission-gear specialist). The Elliotts' experience, as well as that of the other competitive clans, demonstrates that, in NASCAR, "family values" are as much a racing strategy as an ideology.

Generations

Brothers Darrell, left, and Michael Waltrip and the father-son duo of Dale Earnhardt and Dale Earnhardt Jr., above, add to the family flavor of NASCAR Winston Cup Series racing.

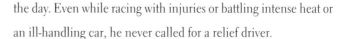

In May of 1975, NASCAR welcomed a new race winner in former Sportsman star Darrell Waltrip, who scored at his "home field," Nashville Fairgrounds Speedway. Waltrip would make noise for many years to come.

The 1975 schedule also saw the arrival of another brash young driver who would make headlines for much of the rest of the century—Dale Earnhardt. On May 25, at Charlotte Motor Speedway, Earnhardt put his car on the grid for the first time in a NASCAR Winston Cup Series race, starting thirty-third in a Dodge owned by Ed Negre. Earnhardt finished twenty-second, forty-five laps behind winner Richard Petty. Earnhardt would not race in a NASCAR Winston Cup car again that season. But the foundation had been put in place. He would be back. With guns blazing.

Challenging Petty and Pearson and, later, Waltrip and Earnhardt was one of the sport's most determined drivers—Cale Yarborough. A few drivers—but only a few—won more races, a few raced for more years, and a few won more money. But friend and foe alike will testify that Yarborough, a son of a struggling South Carolina farmer, was as dogged and persistent as they come on the tight half-miles and high-banked ovals of NASCAR racing. His stubborn refusal to give in to Donnie Allison on the final lap of the 1979 Daytona 500 illustrated his nerve. "I've seen Cale drive cars that I didn't think anybody could drive," said Junior Johnson, whose team built cars for Yarborough for eight seasons ending in 1980. "And he would not quit. There was no end to his willpower."

Yarborough literally never gave up. In a career that stretched across three decades, he never failed to be in his car when it finished

the day. Even while racing with injuries or battling intense heat or an ill-handling car, he never called for a relief driver.

His grit showed through in 1968 when he raced through a steamy South Carolina afternoon to win the Southern 500 at Darlington Raceway, one of his first major triumphs. Darlington is about a dozen miles from Sardis, South Carolina, where Yarborough grew up, and the sun poured down on the old speedway that day like water over a dam. Photographs of Yarborough in victory lane show a weary driver, the grime of a hard race day cloaking his face. Through it all there was a big smile, although Yarborough admitted later that he was so exhausted that he remembers little of what went on in victory lane.

Yarborough signed on with Johnson in 1973 to begin a phenomenal run through the rest of the decade. He won three straight championships from 1976 through 1978, establishing a precedent yet to be matched.

Waltrip horned in on Yarborough's 1977 championship run to win six times and finished fourth in points. The two drivers engaged in one of the fiercest battles of the decade in the Southern 500 that season. Racing for the lead with about a hundred laps remaining, they came upon lapped traffic and had nowhere to run. A huge pileup ensued, and the Waltrip and Yarborough cars were damaged. Upset by the incident, and taking note of the young Waltrip's propensity to talk at length about almost any subject, Yarborough blamed the wreck on "Jaws" Waltrip. It was a nickname that stuck, for a while.

Yarborough was reigning series champion in September 1978 when he and virtually everybody else in NASCAR Winston Cup Series circles participated in one of the biggest parties in the fifty-year history of the series. Although some high-octane celebrations

Flags flying

Left: Dale Earnhardt (center) celebrates a Talladega Superspeedway victory with Kirk Shelmerdine (left) and Richard Childress. NASCAR's champions were celebrated at a party at the White House in September 1978. Opposite: With race cars parked near the White House lawn, drivers Cale Yarborough, (left) David Pearson, and Benny Parsons (right) pose with First Lady Rosalynn Carter, holding a green flag.

have been staged by the more rambunctious members of the NASCAR community over the years, none would top this one. Responding to invitations from President Jimmy Carter, NASCAR drivers, car owners, promoters, and news media representatives gathered on the South Lawn of the White House on September 13 for an evening-long party, an occasion that served to illustrate the sport's new standing. After dining on ham and potato salad at tables decorated in a racing motif, the party-goers enjoyed a concert by singer Willie Nelson and danced into the late hours under a full moon. Four NASCAR Winston Cup Series cars were driven to places of honor in front of the White House. Carter, who had become friends with several drivers, Yarborough in particular while serving as governor of Georgia, missed the party because he was involved in peace talks with Middle East leaders. The event was hosted by First Lady Rosalynn Carter.

The start of the 1979 season marked the debut of the Busch Clash (now the Bud Shootout), a Daytona International Speedway sprint race for NASCAR Winston Cup Series pole position winners from the previous season. The race, which showcases pure speed and driving and drafting skills, quickly became a popular part of February Speedweeks in Daytona. Big-track ace Buddy Baker won the first Clash, averaging a brisk 194.384 mph.

Richard Petty's dramatic victory in the 1979 Daytona 500, scored after the wild last-lap wreck involving Donnie Allison and Cale Yarborough, was the Petty family's second surprise of that Daytona Speedweeks. Kyle Petty, Richard's son, stepped into the racing public eye the weekend before in a two-hundred-mile Automobile Racing Club of America event at Daytona, carrying all the burden of being the King's kid into his first career start. Amazingly, Petty won, starting a huge run of publicity that had reporters speculating that Kyle was ready to follow immediately in the somewhat large footsteps of his father. That trip would have some rough spots, however, and Kyle would smash a few NASCAR Winston Cup cars on the way to his first series victory in 1986.

In the spring of 1979, tough old Darlington Raceway hosted one of NASCAR's classic finishes as Richard Petty and Darrell Waltrip battled while racing in formation over the closing laps of the Rebel 500. Challenging Petty on the ragged edge on one of NASCAR's most formidable tracks, Waltrip won by half a car length.

The race also marked the end of the road for the potent Wood Brothers–David Pearson partnership. An embarrassing pit stop—Pearson, expecting a two-tire change while the crew had loosened all four wheels, left the pits early and banged to a stop when two wheels fell off the car—led to the team's breakup the following week. Alabama driver Neil Bonnett replaced Pearson in the No. 21, and the Woods rolled on, building on their long history in NASCAR racing. Their racing story had begun in 1953 when Glen Wood, the team's owner, drove for the first time at Martinsville Speedway. Leonard Wood, Glen's brother, served as crew chief, and several other family members also worked on the team cars. Glen retired from driving in 1964, but the team remained one of the most effective in NASCAR racing, linking up with some of the sport's greatest drivers—Pearson, Cale Yarborough, Marvin Panch, Curtis Turner, A. J. Foyt, Bonnett, and Dale Jarrett—over the years. Now the team is run by Glen's three children, Eddie, Len, and Kim.

The 1970s ended with Richard Petty bouncing back from a winless 1978 to score five victories and claim his seventh—and last—championship in 1979. He outran Waltrip in the season finale at Ontario (California) Motor Speedway to win the championship by eleven points.

Dale Earnhardt scored a race win and eleven top-five finishes and won the 1979 Rookie of the Year award driving for team owner Rod Osterlund. It would not be the last peak for Earnhardt. Other big moments were coming. And soon.

NASCAR's first generation of racers paved the way for a strong group of drivers who vaulted into superstardom with skill and daring. Davey Allison, top, followed his father, Bobby, into NASCAR Winston Cup Series racing and quickly challenged him for championships. Jeff Burton joined Jack Roush's NASCAR Winston Cup Series team in the second half of the 1990s and became a consistent victory threat and points challenger. Mark Martin, bottom, stormed to the forefront of the sport in the 1990s and became known as a racer's racer. Rusty Wallace, opposite, opened eyes when he finished second in his first NASCAR Winston Cup race in 1980. By the end of the decade, he had almost twenty race wins and a NASCAR Winston Cup championship.

Daredevil Dale

Dale Jarrett became a superhero of sorts in the 1990s, winning the Daytona 500 twice and scoring his first NASCAR Winston Cup Series championship in 1999. Jarrett's generation of drivers carried on the legacy set by the superstars of the 1970s.

Although NASCAR has sanctioned races in widespread parts of the United States since the association's first year of existence, stock car racing's birth in the southeastern part of the country and a long run of success in southern states had earned the sport a sectional label.

Even during the growth boom of the 1960s, NASCAR wrestled with its "southern sport" badge, seeking ways and means to propel stock car racing onto the national stage, to place it in the same category with professional football and basketball and major league baseball. Stretching its wings and its star power, with compelling competition and a cast of aggressive drivers,

NASCAR reached for the world. As a result, by the end of the 1980s the sport had gathered momentum and spread to all corners of the country, shedding its strictly southern image and becoming a sports and entertainment vehicle for fans across America.

As NASCAR grew into new neighborhoods, it formed two partnerships that would become intimately connected with stock car racing's burgeoning progress. First, in the early 1970s, racing was given an immeasurable boost with the arrival of one of NASCAR's major allies: the R.J. Reynolds Tobacco Company. Then cable television came along to join NASCAR's run toward national prominence.

AMERICA'S SPORT

Hooked by cable

Cable television became an active partner with NASCAR in the 1980s, spreading coverage of the sport to homes across America and fueling a new era of growth.

Stock car racing's partnership with television quickly gathered steam after the roaring success of the 1979 Daytona 500 broadcast, but the alliance wouldn't reach full flower until the growth of cable networks in the 1980s brought media players like ESPN and TNN onto the scene.

Television was dominated by the Big Three networks—CBS, NBC, and ABC—in 1979 when ESPN, then known as the Entertainment and Sports Programming Network, started broadcasting. The Connecticut-based network, formed with the idea that enough was happening in the sports world to fill time on a twenty-four-hour, all-sports channel, needed programming—in bunches. Its first live event was a professional slow-pitch softball game. ESPN soon hooked up with NASCAR, and the two rode along like cars in a Daytona draft. The Nashville Network and Turner Broadcasting System also became NASCAR partners, and soon every NASCAR Winston Cup Series race was being shown live, start to finish. It was a far cry from the days of the 1960s, when bits and pieces of races made television's programming lists. And television's growing impact on the sport stretched far beyond NASCAR's drivers, teams, speedways, and fans. National television exposure became a bonanza for companies interested in sponsoring race teams and lending their names to titles of races, and everyone— the drivers, NASCAR, the sponsoring corporations, television, and the fans—prospered.

Television helped carry the NASCAR message to new frontiers, spreading the sport's foundation and strengthening its presence in areas that previously had little touch with major league motorsports.

In November 1999, NASCAR took one of the most important steps in its history, signing a contract with NBC, Fox, TBS, and the fx Network for broadcast coverage of its NASCAR Winston Cup Series and NASCAR Busch Series, Grand National Division races beginning with the 2001 season. The new package, the mastermind of Bill France Jr., Brian France, and NASCAR's vice president of broadcasting Bray Cary, lifted NASCAR into the same broadcast arena as other major American sports, and gave NASCAR racing the network platform it needed to push toward the future.

Through such a consolidation NASCAR was able to provide fans strong consistency in the scheduling of NASCAR programming, and allowed fans easier access to NASCAR racing broadcasts. And through aggressive on-air promotion, similar to the NBA and NFL, NASCAR can expand its reach to include the casual sports fan as well as loyal motorsports followers. NASCAR could then begin to offer fans Internet and digital television products that had not been previously available.

But long before television's impact was felt, the organization the France family built arrived at a critical juncture. As the 1960s turned into the '70s and Bill France Sr. gave control of NASCAR to Bill France Jr., times were changing. Car manufacturers in Detroit were pulling away from the sport (at least officially), and the big "factory" money that had bolstered racing through much of the 1960s began to dissipate. The past and its colorful days of barnstorming dirt-track racers were pulling the sport in one direction; the superspeedway boom of the '60s was pulling in another. NASCAR had the product to go truly national, but many still saw the sport as largely southern.

All-seeing eye

The Nashville Network and other cable television entities gave live coverage to every race on the NASCAR schedule.

Live, from everywhere

As a brand-new network with a full twenty-four hours each day to fill, ESPN needed NASCAR. The marriage produced good things for both partners.

Events of December 1970 ignited the series of changes that provided NASCAR racing with the ladder it needed to climb to the highest levels of American sports and to gain the attention of television executives.

Oddly enough, the sequence of events began with a seemingly unrelated action: the federal government's decision to ban tobacco advertising from television. Tobacco companies suddenly had millions of promotional dollars to spend in other arenas.

Junior Johnson, then a Grand National team owner, pitched a car sponsorship proposal to representatives of R.J. Reynolds, headquartered in Winston-Salem, North Carolina. Johnson later said he quickly realized that RJR had bigger things in mind, and he suggested a meeting with NASCAR. Bill France Sr. and Jr. met with Reynolds officials, leading to a December 1970 announcement that the company would put the full strength of its marketing and public relations efforts behind NASCAR's Grand National series.

Since Reynolds's 1970 announcement, the red and white colors of Winston cigarettes have been virtually as important to NASCAR racing as the black and white of the checkered flag. And the money stream that began that month in Winston-Salem turned into a river of opportunity for NASCAR, its drivers, its teams, and—in more ways than one—its fans.

The first items on the agenda were sponsorship of what would become the Winston 500 at Talladega, Alabama, and a $100,000 addition to the series point fund. NASCAR Grand National racing became NASCAR Winston Cup Grand National racing, and, later, simply the NASCAR Winston Cup Series. Men and women in bright red and white shirts and suits, and with public relations training in the respected RJR tradition, began showing up at races to help in promotions, and thousands of gallons of red and white paint were sent to tracks to spruce up their fences, pit walls, buildings, and signs.

Ralph Seagraves, RJR's point man on the NASCAR project, was a key player in its launch and its early success. T. Wayne Robertson became Seagraves's understudy (and later his successor) in the operation, and both brought vibrant ideas to the job.

Besides the great infusion of money and marketing expertise, RJR is given credit for opening the NASCAR door to nonautomotive sponsorships, yet another vehicle the sport used to spread its message into new markets. Before Winston, virtually all significant racing

sponsorships were provided by companies that produced automotive products. Reynolds proved that attaching its product names to motorsports worked as a sales and marketing vehicle, and many other companies would follow. From the old days on southern dirt tracks, when "Joe's Service Station" might be painted on the quarter-panel of a race car, the sport had moved into a new world where "Tide," "Gatorade," and "Wrangler" became car identifiers.

A prominent nonautomotive sponsor, Anheuser-Busch, Inc., began sponsoring two popular touring series that are still run today. The Busch North Series features cars that are very similar to the full-bodied sedans that run in the NASCAR Busch Series, with minor exceptions in tires, engines, and weight factors. The series features competition on a string of tracks that stretch from Maine to western Pennsylvania and gives some of the Northeast's best drivers opportunities to race on superspeedways, road courses, and short tracks. Some of the region's most historic tracks, including Watkins Glen International, Nazareth Speedway in Pennsylvania, and Stafford Motor Speedway in Connecticut, host the series. The tour has produced such drivers as Mike Stefanik, Andy Santerre, and Ricky Craven. The Busch All-Star Series gives a midwestern flavor to NASCAR's Touring Division. NASCAR's

Billboards, large and small

The arrival of the R.J. Reynolds Tobacco Company as primary series sponsor created new interest in NASCAR Winston Cup Series racing among nontraditional sponsors. Proctor and Gamble jumped at the chance to advertise its Tide detergent brand through a sponsorship with the Darrell Waltrip team, opposite.

only dirt track touring series, the All-Star circuit visits more than a dozen tracks in Nebraska, Iowa, Illinois, and South Dakota. Nebraska brothers Steve and Joe Kosiski have been dominant forces on the tour in recent seasons.

Also started up in the mid-1980s, the Raybestos Northwest Series has been entertaining fans in the Northwestern corner of the United States for fifteen years. NASCAR Winston Cup Series drivers Derrike Cope and Chad Little and Busch Grand National drivers Jeff Krogh and Mark Krogh learned the trade on Northwest Series tracks. A similar tour—the Featherlite Southwest Series—covers speedways in California, Nevada, Arizona, and Colorado, and builds points each season toward a championship. The series' tracks range from small (1/3-mile) to large (2.52 miles).

With the potent new mix of television, Fortune 500 sponsors, and strong marketing input from NASCAR, the sport kicked into a higher gear. Television ratings boomed, attendance numbers grew, and grandstands became more diverse (with more and more women and a broader sweep of middle America attending races). Race sites became favorite spots for sponsoring companies to host clients, employees, and friends as NASCAR racing evolved into a dominant force in the world of marketing.

In the 1980s, NASCAR finally stepped forward to take its place alongside the other big guns of the American sports landscape. At the core of this explosion of interest and investment in racing was a new wave of competition, one sparked by drivers like Buddy Baker, Benny Parsons, and Dale Earnhardt, who would use the last twenty years of the century to write a compelling motorsports story rivaled by few others.

The 1980 season produced an early highlight as Baker, an acknowledged master of big-track racing but stuck with a long history of bad luck at Daytona, finally won the Daytona 500 after years of "almosts" in NASCAR's biggest race. He averaged a sizzling 177.602 mph, a record speed.

The season's first visit to Charlotte provided a showcase for Parsons and Darrell Waltrip in the longest race of the year, the World 600. Near the end of a grueling day, they raced like they were fresh out of the chute, swapping the lead eight times in the final twenty-six laps, Parsons edging out front by about five feet at the finish. It was the sort of racing television loved, providing an excellent example of the type of competitive action NASCAR was generating week after week, drawing thousands of new fans into the mix.

The dawning of the 1980s placed Earnhardt front and center of NASCAR Winston Cup Series racing. He had shown surprising promise in 1979, winning the rookie of the year race and becoming one of a handful of drivers to score a victory in their first season. Pit road roamers were eager to see what he could do in his second season, and his partnership with California businessman Rod Osterlund, also new to racing but with resources that built a very competitive team, placed him in position to perform.

That he did.

Racing no less a personage than the King himself—Richard Petty, at the top of the point standings—Earnhardt soared in the 1980 season, bringing pride to the home folks on the mill hill in Kannapolis, North Carolina, on the way to five victories and the NASCAR Winston Cup Series championship. The square-shouldered, skinny kid, not that many months removed from a hand-to-mouth existence in the tough world of short-track Sportsman racing, had shot to the top quickly. In only his second full year at the highest level of stock car racing, Earnhardt was the boss, already a champion and a driver of unlimited potential.

It took only a few months for the Earnhardt freight train to derail, however. Osterlund unexpectedly sold his team midway through the 1981 season, and a wealthy Kentucky coal mine operator named Jim Stacy took over. Earnhardt and Stacy did not mesh, and Earnhardt left the team after only four races under the new ownership, taking his Wrangler sponsorship to the team of veteran racer Richard Childress, who had decided to end his driving career and concentrate on operating a team. Childress provided a sort of

A comet, burning brightly

With a brash style and the heart of a charger, Tim Richmond recharged memories of the bold racers of NASCAR's early years.

"safety valve" rescue spot for the frustrated Earnhardt. Neither man could have imagined the heights they eventually would reach.

NASCAR racing was also attracting new competitors, in particular strong drivers from other forms of racing. Making his first appearance on the NASCAR Winston Cup scene in 1980 was a young open-wheel driver from northern Ohio named Tim Richmond. Although he drove five races for team owner D. K. Ulrich without reaching the top ten in any of them, alert observers could see "star" written on Richmond. After a 1981 season in which he bounced around from ride to ride, he scored two victories in 1982, attracting the attention of more established operations. He drove the next three seasons for Raymond Beadle, winning two races and earning a spot in Rick Hendrick–owned cars for 1986. It was there that Richmond realized his promise, winning seven times while battling mightily with the entrenched stars of the day.

> NASCAR officials had overseen a racing circuit that featured monster muscle cars. After gas prices rocketed in the mid-1970s, attitudes changed.

Richmond's career ended early. He drove his last race in 1987 and died from health complications on August 13, 1989. He is remembered as a different sort of driver, one who dressed in expensive suits and did things his way, but one who also sparked memories of racers like Curtis Turner and Junior Johnson with a daring, go-for-broke driving style.

The 1981 season presented a significant hurdle for NASCAR officials, even as they celebrated the sport's growing popularity and new national presence. Not too many years earlier, they had overseen a racing circuit that featured monster muscle cars— winged beasts like Plymouth Superbirds and Dodge Daytonas, vehicles that were as big and brawny as Detroit's imagination. Then, after gasoline prices rocketed in the mid-1970s, attitudes changed. Americans were driving smaller cars, and NASCAR—ever mindful of the edict of founder Bill France Sr. that its racers should compete in cars similar to those sitting in the driveways of middle America—responded on its speedways.

In 1981, the wheelbase of NASCAR Winston Cup Series cars was trimmed from 115 inches to 110, bringing cars like the Buick Regal, the Pontiac Grand Prix, the Ford Thunderbird, and the Dodge Mirada into the realm of NASCAR eligibility. Drivers and mechanics went from knowing almost everything about their race cars to knowing very little. Off-season tests proved that the smaller cars would be tricky to maneuver and difficult to set up properly. After several crashes in practice and races leading to the Daytona 500 in February, NASCAR officials made changes in rear-deck spoiler height to make the new cars more stable. The hit of Speedweeks at Daytona was a Pontiac LeMans driven by Bobby Allison, whose team had fine-tuned the new model in secret tests and surprised the competition with a car that was both rapid and reliable.

The competitive posture of the new cars was underlined several times during that season, perhaps with no greater authority than in the Talladega 500 in Alabama. In one of the greatest finishes in motorsports history, rookie Ron Bouchard slipped past Terry Labonte and Darrell Waltrip coming out of the last turn on the last lap and beat them to the finish line by a few inches in a three-abreast drag race. The win was Bouchard's only NASCAR Winston Cup Series victory. His father, who had been watching the race at home in Massachusetts, missed the finish because of television technical problems. He practically destroyed his television in frustration.

Downsizing

The wheelbase of NASCAR Winston Cup Series cars dropped from 115 inches to 110 for the 1981 season, making cars like Junior Johnson's successful Buick Regal eligible at NASCAR's highest level.

A new generation of fans

As NASCAR moved into national prominence in the 1980s,
a new legion of youngsters joined the ranks of fans.

The 1981 season produced another landmark that accelerated NASCAR's push to give its racing a broader national base. NASCAR officials moved the season-ending NASCAR Winston Cup Series awards banquet from its traditional Daytona Beach home to New York City, thus gaining an important foothold in the news media capital of the world. Since December 1981, NASCAR's best and brightest have traveled to New York to pick up their season-ending trophies and awards checks, giving the NASCAR Winston Cup Series invaluable exposure. It was another step forward in the growth pattern.

Accepting the first NASCAR Winston Cup trophy awarded in New York was Darrell Waltrip, who would rule most of the early 1980s. He and team owner Junior Johnson combined for championship runs in 1981, '82, and '85. Waltrip was particularly strong in the '81 and '82 seasons, recording twelve victories each year. A controversial figure in his early racing years, in part because he never hesitated to speak his mind on any of a number of subjects, Waltrip settled into superstardom as one of the "good guys" of the NASCAR Winston Cup Series circuit in the closing years of the 1980s and proved his abilities time and again in an increasingly competitive climate. He reached one of the peaks of his career in the 1989 Daytona 500, finally winning NASCAR's biggest race after seventeen years of trying. Among the results was one of the most exuberant victory lane celebrations in the track's thirty-year history.

Richard Petty, whose track superiority Waltrip and other younger drivers were challenging, saw his driving career hit an uncharacteristic low October 10, 1983, at Charlotte Motor Speedway. Barely competitive in the National 500 most of the day, Petty charged from the rear late in the race and stunned the crowd by winning by three seconds. The No. 43 team's secrets became all too obvious after the race. The crew had put left-side tires on the right side of the car during a pit stop, a definite rules violation. And that was only the beginning. Officials discovered during the postrace teardown that the engine in Petty's car measured 382 cubic inches,

significantly larger than the 358 allowed. After much discussion, Petty was allowed to keep the victory, but he was fined a then-record $35,000 and penalized eighty-four NASCAR Winston Cup Series points.

At Talladega in 1984, the sweep of NASCAR competition was underlined yet again. The Winston 500 saw a remarkable seventy-five lead changes in an ultracompetitive event, establishing a NASCAR Winston Cup record. Thirteen drivers held the lead on the superfast afternoon as traffic swept around the monster speedway at speeds over 200 mph. Cale Yarborough emerged as the winner.

The car—a beautiful, bright red and blue No. 43 Pontiac— is now in the Smithsonian Institution. Then, in the hot summer of 1984, it was in Cale Yarborough's face, and the race finish in which it participated became one of NASCAR's landmarks, perfectly illustrating stock car racing's rush toward national prominence.

On one of the most memorable days of Richard Petty's storied racing career, July 4, 1984, he scored his two-hundredth victory and entertained the president of the United States at the same time. There would be no more wins for Petty after that afternoon, making the moment in the Daytona sun even more special as the years rolled by.

Daytona International Speedway and NASCAR officials knew weeks before that President Ronald Reagan would be in attendance at

A special ride

Richard Petty drove this Pontiac to his two-hundredth victory on July 4, 1984. The car later was donated to the Smithsonian Institution.

the Firecracker 400 that July. It marked the first time that a U.S. president had attended a NASCAR Winston Cup Series race while in office. Security officials made significant changes to normal race-day operations to accommodate the president and his entourage.

Petty and Yarborough put on the sort of show the day demanded. Each led dozens of laps in steamy conditions at the track. With the final laps counting down, they were one-two. Doug Heveron crashed with two laps to go, bringing out the caution flag. When Petty and Yarborough saw the yellow caution lights blinking, they knew the race would end under caution and that their race to the finish line on the caution lap would determine the day's winner. They roared side by side through the tri-oval, Petty low and Yarborough high, bumping sheet metal at 200 mph as they raced to the line. Petty won by a few feet, much to the amazement of the president, who had participated in the radio broadcast of the race and was watching high above the stands as the two NASCAR Winston Cup Series superstars wrestled for first place.

> They roared side by side through the tri-oval, Petty low and Yarborough high, bumping sheet metal at 200 mph as they raced to the line.

The aftermath of the finish created one of the great NASCAR Winston Cup Series trivia questions. Many fans assume that Yarborough finished second in the race because he was side by side with Petty on the most important lap of the day. But Harry Gant actually took second, because Yarborough, momentarily thinking the race was over when he lost the chase to Petty, pulled into the garage area, ignoring the final lap. He quickly returned to the track, but Gant beat him to the line on the last lap.

After the race, Reagan dined with drivers and their families in the Daytona garage.

Helping to construct NASCAR's growth spiral in the 1980s was the introduction of The Winston, a big-bucks, big-stars special event that was a hit from the beginning. It wasn't an entirely new concept. NASCAR had an "all-star race" as early as February 19, 1961, when Joe Weatherly won the ten-lap American Challenge

Cup, a special event at Daytona International Speedway. Weatherly, one of eleven drivers in the race, won one thousand dollars. But ears perked up around the sport in 1985 when series sponsor R.J. Reynolds announced the creation of The Winston, a sprint race for race winners from the previous season. The biggest news was the money involved. First place for the seventy-lap, 105-mile race at Charlotte Motor Speedway would pay $200,000, a healthy check for a short day's work.

The first race, held May 25, 1985, at Charlotte, had spots for a dozen drivers. Darrell Waltrip outran Harry Gant with two laps to go and won the race by .31 of a second. A heartbeat after crossing the checkered flag, the engine in Waltrip's car exploded, producing a big plume of smoke.

The Winston has produced a string of wild moments that have had fans in an uproar, opposite. In 1987, Dale Earnhardt and Bill Elliott had a major confrontation along the Charlotte Motor Speedway frontstretch, shown above in 1996, forcing Earnhardt onto the grass bordering the track. He recovered quickly and went on to win the race. Two years later, Rusty Wallace bumped Darrell Waltrip and sent Waltrip's car spinning near the end of the race, opening the door for a controversial Wallace victory. In 1995, Earnhardt and Waltrip crashed while wrestling for the lead, paving the way for Jeff Gordon to finish first.

Over the next fifteen years, The Winston would undergo several format changes, the rules for eligibility would be modified, and the venue would be moved—for one season only—to Atlanta Motor Speedway. But the race often produced riveting drama and slam-bang finishes. When Charlotte Motor Speedway added lights and moved the event to evening hours in 1992, it gained an extra layer of excitement, and record crowds flocked to the speedway to enjoy the spectacle.

The finish of that first night race perhaps was the peak of The Winston's first fifteen years. On the final lap, Dale Earnhardt drove low in the third turn to challenge leader Kyle Petty. Petty forced him even lower, and Earnhardt went into a spin. Davey Allison avoided Earnhardt and surged past Petty in the final moments, their cars banging together near the start-finish line. Allison took the checkered flag in a shower of sparks, then slammed his car into the outside wall. The Ford received heavy damage, and Allison missed the victory lane ceremonies because he was transported to a nearby hospital for overnight observation.

The legend of The Winston grew with each passing year. Its dramatic finishes and unusual format drew new fans to racing, particularly via television.

Bill Elliott, winner of The Winston in 1986 and one of racing's biggest stars in the 1980s, came out of the north Georgia mountains with one thing on his mind: driving at motorsports' highest level. A successful short-tracker with his family-owned team,

Bill Elliott's 1985 season electrified the sport and had teams up and down pit road scratching their collective head in wonder.

Elliott, a tall, lanky, rather shy sort, had shown the ability very early to understand the often complex relationship between a race car chassis and the surfaces it must cross. He both worked on and drove the cars he raced, a combination quite common for young drivers, but this red-haired Georgian seemed to adapt to it much better than most.

Elliott's underfinanced family team raced part time for several NASCAR Winston Cup Series seasons (beginning in 1976) before hooking up with Harry Melling, who brought new resources to the operation. Elliott won for the first time in 1983, scored three victories in 1984, and then, in 1985, had the magical sort of season that most racers see only in their dreams. The Elliott team hit on a winning formula on the circuit's big tracks that season and was virtually invincible, notching eleven superspeedway victories, several by comfortable margins. Three of those wins came in the Daytona 500, the Winston 500, and the Southern 500, giving Elliott the Winston Million in its first season. He finished the year with $2.4 million in winnings, more than four times his previous high.

Elliott's 1985 season electrified the sport and had teams up and down pit road scratching their collective head in wonder. Elliott's dominance led to an early-season rules change by NASCAR, as officials tried to bring Elliott and his struggling chasers closer together. But Elliott was a rocket on the tour's first visit of the season to Talladega, running a record qualifying lap of 209.398 mph. An early-race pit stop for a faulty oil fitting cost Elliott almost two laps, but his car was so strong that he made up the distance under green-flag conditions and rolled to a comfortable victory. It was one of the most amazing big-track performances in NASCAR history.

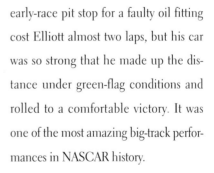

Million Dollar Bill

Bill Elliott answered the R.J. Reynolds Tobacco Company's million-dollar challenge in 1985, winning three major superspeedway races to collect the huge bonus in the first season of the Winston Million program.

Bill Elliott watched faux dollar bills float down around him in the frenzy of a wild victory-lane celebration at the Southern 500 at Darlington Raceway on September 1, 1985.

It was Elliott's moment as he toasted the occasion of winning the Winston Million bonus, but the day also served as a very visible reminder to other drivers of the treasure chest series sponsor R.J. Reynolds had left at their front door.

The word million became part of everyday vocabulary in NASCAR Winston Cup Series garage areas.

Reynolds began offering the Winston Million in 1985. The huge bonus was available to any driver who could win three of the so-called Big Four races—Daytona 500, Winston 500, Coca-Cola 600, and Southern 500. The possibility of awarding the prize was considered slim. Reynolds's officials

were genuinely surprised when Elliott stepped to the plate and won it in the first year it was offered.

Elliott was the dominant driver of 1985. His team won eleven races on superspeedways that season, making the Georgia driver a prime contender for the big money. Elliott won the Daytona 500 to open the season and then rallied to win at Talladega in May, putting him in position to win the million at Charlotte (later in May) or Darlington in September.

Elliott stumbled at Charlotte, finishing eighteenth after experiencing tire and brake trouble. Darlington, in the hot and humid final weeks of summer, was his last shot.

Money machine

Monster checks became the order of the day as R.J. Reynolds, through its Winston brand, sponsored special incentive programs for drivers—and for fans. Several fans joined million-dollar winners Jeff Gordon, Dale Jarrett, and Jeff Burton through a national sweepstakes drawing that paired fans with drivers in the race for $1 million.

During Southern 500 week, the Elliott team arranged for additional garage-area security so the work necessary for a shot at victory could be performed. It paid off—and so did Winston. Despite challenges by Dale Earnhardt, Harry Gant, and Cale Yarborough, Elliott won by about a second, sparking a wild celebration in the grandstands and, later, in victory lane.

The Winston Million prize would go uncollected for a dozen seasons after Elliott's inaugural score.

In 1997, Jeff Gordon added spice to a ten-win championship season by becoming the second driver to claim the million in what became its final year. Gordon won in impressive fashion at Daytona, Charlotte, and Darlington to add the huge paycheck to a seasonal dollar total that would surpass $6 million.

For the 1998 season, in part to help NASCAR celebrate its fiftieth year, R.J. Reynolds replaced the Winston Million program with a new big-bucks extravaganza: the Winston No Bull 5. The No Bull 5 greatly expanded the list of eligible drivers, inflated the money totals they could win, and brought NASCAR Winston Cup fans into the picture.

The Daytona 500, Coca-Cola 600, Brickyard 400, Southern 500, and Winston 500 were designated as No Bull 5 races. If any of the top five drivers in the previous No Bull 5 event won the next race in the series, that driver—and a fan paired with him through a sweepstakes drawing—won $1 million.

Gordon collected the money twice in 1998, and Dale Jarrett scored once.

Jeff Burton won twice and Gordon won once as the program was continued in 1999 with a similar format and a new track, Las Vegas Motor Speedway.

To the bank

Jeff Burton, above, and Dale Jarrett were among the drivers cashing million-dollar checks in the 1990s as part of Winston's No Bull 5 program.

The season thrust Elliott into the international motorsports spotlight. He was satisfied working on his cars and winning a race now and then, but his stunning success made him the target of virtually every reporter with a pen and every television station with a camera. He admitted he wasn't comfortable with his fame and sometimes escaped into his team's hauler to get away from everything.

Elliott earned fans by the millions. His fast driving and slow Georgia drawl endeared him to increasing numbers of spectators, and he was named NASCAR's most popular driver fourteen times, so often that it became almost standard operating procedure for him to win the award.

Elliott raced with Melling for ten years, reaching a peak by winning the NASCAR Winston Cup Series championship in 1988 before joining team owner Junior Johnson for three seasons, then returned to his north Georgia roots to rebuild his own team in 1995.

Among those wrestling Elliott for dominance in the 1980s was Bobby Allison, who decided he wanted to be a stock car racer when he saw a Florida short-track race as a teenager. Allison became one of the greatest drivers in the history of motorsports, building a reputation as one of the fiercest, most determined competitors to ever take a green flag. He went up against the best of his day—Richard Petty, Cale Yarborough, Darrell Waltrip, David Pearson, Bill Elliott— and never turned away from a challenge, winning eighty-four times on the toughest stock car circuit in the world and

> **Fiercely independent, Allison wanted things done his way, a trait that sometimes caused him to move on to other pastures despite success.**

enjoying some of his peak seasons as the sport gained new luster nationally.

Mixed with Allison's glorious highs, however, were staggering losses. His younger son, Clifford, lost his life in a practice session accident at Michigan Speedway. His older son, Davey, also died. Allison himself had a brush with death in 1988, suffering debilitating injuries in an accident at Pocono Raceway and then embarking on a grueling, years-long rehabilitation that sapped his energies but didn't blunt his resolve.

Bobby Allison and his brother Donnie raced on Florida short tracks with considerable success before moving to Alabama, which offered bigger purses and the hospitality of the little village of Hueytown, which the Allisons and other successful racers turned into a motorsports capital. Soon there were enough of them—Red Farmer and Neil Bonnett were other principals—to form a quite unofficial but very formidable group known as the Alabama Gang.

Bobby won four championships in NASCAR Modified racing, NASCAR's oldest division of race cars that was formalized into the Featherlite Modified Series in the early 1980s. The NASCAR Winston Cup Series was his dream, though, and he moved into the series with little more than his pieced-together race car and a powerful will to win. He won six races in his own cars—three in 1966 and three in '67—before moving into numerous partnerships with other team owners, including Cotton Owens, Bud Moore, Holman-Moody, Mario Rossi, Junior Johnson, Roger Penske, and DiGard Racing. Fiercely independent, Allison wanted things done his way, a trait that sometimes caused him to move on to other pastures despite success, most notably after he and Johnson teamed to win ten races in 1972. After only one season, Allison left Johnson to race his own cars again.

Allison drove DiGard Racing Buicks prepared by Gary Nelson, now the NASCAR Winston Cup Series director, and powered by

Alabama Gang leader

Bobby Allison, here wrapped to protect a rib injury, was one of the NASCAR Winston Cup Series' most determined and talented drivers. He won eighty-four times.

Bobby Allison led his son, Davey, to the checkered flag in
the 1988 Daytona 500, a finish that would become even
more special a few months later when the older Allison's
career ended early because of an accident.

engines built by Robert Yates, now a top series team owner, to the NASCAR Winston Cup Series championship in 1983, finally reaching a goal he had established back in the early 1960s when he struggled to find enough car parts to get to the racetrack. By the time the Pocono wreck forced him into retirement, he had won almost everything there was to win, reaching a victory level matched by only three other drivers.

Allison and the men he raced against drove under new regulations at the tour's biggest tracks beginning in the 1987 season. Speeds had escalated through much of the 1980s, parallelling NASCAR's national rise—Benny Parsons registered the first official 200-mph qualifying lap (200.176) in April 1982 at Talladega—and peaked with Bill Elliott's 212-mph qualifying lap at Talladega in April 1987. In the interest of safety, NASCAR sought ways to slow cars. That search resulted in the use of smaller carburetors in the summer of 1987 and the return of carburetor restrictor plates in 1988. The restrictor plates have been in use at Talladega and Daytona since 1988 and have been a major component in NASCAR's drive to limit speeds at its biggest superspeedways.

The 1980s also marked the arrival of several new team owners who would play important roles in the ongoing elevation of NASCAR racing to new levels. Chief among them was Rick

The 1980s marked the arrival of several team owners who would play major roles in the ongoing elevation of NASCAR racing to new levels.

Hendrick, very successful in the business of selling automobiles and hungering for the same sort of achievement racing them. Hendrick started in 1984 with a one-car operation for driver Geoff Bodine, but soon expanded to two and later three cars, bringing in drivers Tim Richmond, Darrell Waltrip, Benny Parsons, Ken Schrader, and Ricky Rudd, among others, to race for him. Hendrick's greatest success would be reached in the 1990s when he signed young Jeff Gordon to start a team that would develop into a dynasty in only a few years. Terry Labonte, a crafty veteran driver from Texas, also would drive Hendrick's Chevrolets to championship success.

Joining Hendrick on the team ownership list in the 1980s were Larry McClure, Harry Melling, Chuck Rider, Jack Roush, Felix Sabates, and Robert Yates, a group of very different men, all of whom had a significant impact as NASCAR competition changed from domination by a few teams in the 1970s to a more diverse landscape.

A major force in team ownership in the 1980s—and beyond—was journeyman driver Richard Childress, who raced his own cars with limited success through most of the 1970s. He gave up driving to put young racer Dale Earnhardt in the seat of his cars two-thirds through the 1981 season, starting a relationship that would soon turn golden.

Earnhardt left Childress for two seasons but returned in 1984, resuming an ongoing relationship that has resulted in dozens of victories and six NASCAR Winston Cup Series championships (Earnhardt won another title separate from Childress). The victory-lane visits that had escaped Childress as a driver for his own underfunded

Building an empire

Opposite: Richard Childress, with driver Mike Skinner (right), struggled with an underfinanced operation during his driving years but found success as a team owner with Skinner and Dale Earnhardt. Childress also was among several NASCAR Winston Cup competitors who built teams for the new NASCAR Craftsman Truck Series, left.

operation now came in waves, and both men rose to become key forces in NASCAR's ascension.

As talented and forceful drivers like Waltrip, Earnhardt, and later, Gordon came on the scene to drive NASCAR to new levels of marketing, television, and attendance growth, the NASCAR Winston Cup circuit needed bigger facilities to house the new fan numbers. The days of viewing NASCAR as a southern regional sport were well in the past, and increasing numbers of fans wanted to see the evolving sport and its daredevil cast of drivers.

They came to places like Bristol Motor Speedway in the Appalachian Mountains of eastern Tennessee. Bristol serves as a prime example of the spectacular growth that NASCAR has enjoyed through the 1980s and '90s.

Opened in 1961, Bristol struggled for several years. Built as a half-mile oval during a period of superspeedway emphasis, the little track had crowds of less than ten thousand for some of its early events. In 1969, the track was refurbished, its twenty-two-degree banking increased to thirty-six degrees, the most severe in NASCAR racing. The immediate effect was to create a racing "bowl," a superfast half-mile that would push drivers to sensational speeds for a short track. In 1978, the track's August NASCAR Winston Cup Series race was moved from afternoon to night, creating an entirely new racing environment. "We wanted something cool for the fans, cooler on the drivers, and something that would be a different spectacle," said former track co-owner Lanny Hester. "We thought the night race would be a concept we could promote." It was an understatement. The night race was an immediate hit, drawing a crowd of more than twenty-five thousand compared to only twelve thousand the year before in the August afternoon heat. "It was one of the high points of my career, of my lifetime, really, to be involved in something that was such a major turnaround," said Ed Clark, then the Bristol track's public relations director, now president of Atlanta Motor Speedway.

> "We wanted something cool for the fans and cooler on the drivers that would be a different spectacle."
> —TRACK OWNER LANNY HESTER

Racing took on a new shine—literally—at night. "I remember people talking about how the brakes glowed," said former driver Cale Yarborough. "People who have never seen night racing were amazed about how the brakes turned cherry red and stayed that way. I guess they figured everybody would tear their brakes up because they were red hot."

Bristol soon became one of the hottest tickets in motorsports. In the 1990s, new owner Bruton Smith started a building program that pushed seating capacity to almost 150,000, and the track that had trouble drawing 10,000 fans in the 1970s became one of the great success stories of NASCAR.

A check of license plates in the sprawling parking areas outside the track—or any track on the NASCAR Winston Cup schedule—would reveal a list of spectators from dozens of states and every region of the country. From the tight half-mile at Bristol to the long backstretch at Daytona and beyond, NASCAR had become America's sport, bringing its history of close competition and universally appealing drivers to an ever-growing fan base.

The highway to the future was wide open.

Under the lights

Night racing gives the NASCAR Winston Cup Series a new flair, putting fire in the night sky and, occasionally, on the asphalt, as evidenced by evening action at Bristol, above, and Richmond, opposite.

The field forms for action at Richmond International
Raceway, a three-quarter-mile track that has been a part
of NASCAR since the 1950s.

New man in town

A success in other forms of racing, Jack Roush, opposite, entered the NASCAR Winston Cup Series in 1988 and soon had a winner in Mark Martin. Above: Jeff Burton (No. 99) joined the team in 1996 and gave Roush three victories the next season.

Although the NASCAR Winston Cup Series is rightfully recognized as the number-one venue for auto racing in the world, it is far from alone in the wide world of NASCAR. Lined up alongside the flagship NASCAR Winston Cup circuit are other racing series that give the sanctioning body a wide spectrum of competition, provide entry points for drivers of varying talent levels, and generate motorsports entertainment for fans across the country.

At the top of the list are the NASCAR Busch Series, Grand National Division and the NASCAR Craftsman Truck Series, circuits that carry the NASCAR flag from East Coast to West Coast and into several racing hotbeds that aren't visited by NASCAR Winston Cup racing.

The NASCAR Busch Series originated in 1982 when NASCAR gave substantial credibility and financial boosts to the former Late Model Sportsman (LMS) series, a predominantly short-track division that had produced some of NASCAR Winston Cup's top stars and showcased hard-nosed bullring kings like Harry Gant, Sam Ard, Jack Ingram, Tommy Ellis, and Butch Lindley. LMS became Busch Grand National, immediately gaining the considerable financial support of Anheuser-Busch, Inc. and the

visibility of a new, more demanding schedule, with more of an emphasis on superspeedway racing.

Over years of development, the NASCAR Busch Series settled into a comfortable niche as a stepping-stone for drivers on the way up to the NASCAR Winston Cup Series and for journeyman competitors who didn't necessarily want the challenge of NASCAR Winston Cup competition but were looking for a high-profile, competitive circuit for full-bodied stock cars.

Racing into the 1990s, the NASCAR Busch Series also became a venue for NASCAR Winston Cup regulars. Many drive NASCAR Busch Series (NBS) cars in weekend companion events, gaining exposure for their sponsors and providing another part of the learning curve for those NBS drivers who follow their tracks around speedways. Although it has smaller horsepower and wheelbase numbers, the NASCAR Busch Series gives drivers a very representative look—on many of the same tracks—at what it would be like to race a NASCAR Winston Cup car.

Development of the NASCAR Craftsman Truck Series in 1994 filled a niche in NASCAR circles. The accelerating growth of NASCAR created a need for another top series to assist in driver development, and America's love affair with trucks made a racing series for pickups a no-brainer.

Different strokes

NASCAR continues to stretch its boundaries, broadening the schedule for its NASCAR Busch Series, above, and giving drivers another avenue to explore with the NASCAR Craftsman Truck Series, below.

Officials looked out into the parking lots of NASCAR events and saw practically as many pickups as cars, so the concept of racing tough trucks like Ford F-150s, Dodge Rams, and Chevy Silverados made a lot of sense.

NASCAR President Bill France Jr. announced the creation of the series in May 1994, and four demonstration races were held that year to showcase the series' possibilities.

The Craftsman Truck Series debuted February 5, 1995, at Phoenix International Raceway, with Mike Skinner edging Terry Labonte. The series gave career boosts to Skinner, Ron Hornaday, Jack Sprague, Kenny Irwin, and several other drivers, and consistently produced some of the closest racing in all of NASCAR.

As NASCAR prepared for the new millennium, there were plenty of other opportunities for drivers to test their skills under the NASCAR banner.

The NASCAR Winston West Series originated in 1954, a few years after NASCAR's birth. As part of the NASCAR Touring Division, the circuit includes short tracks and superspeedways and stretches from the West Coast to Japan. The NASCAR Goody's Dash Series and NASCAR Slim Jim All-Pro Series, which both bring small-track racing to the Southeast, offer fierce competition for smaller cars and also have a competitive mix of young drivers and more experienced veterans. The northeastern NASCAR Featherlite Modified Series, NASCAR's oldest series and once home to such greats as Richie Evans and Jerry Cook, continues to showcase tight competition among powerful, low-slung Modified racers. Filling the demand for racing across the country are other NASCAR touring circuits: the NASCAR Busch North Series; the midwestern NASCAR Busch All-Star Series; the NASCAR RE/MAX Challenge Series, which brings NASCAR Winston Cup–style racing to the northern Midwest; the NASCAR Featherlite Southwest Series; and the NASCAR Raybestos Brakes Northwest Series.

The NASCAR Weekly Racing Series provides drivers from all over the country with local, regional, and national recognition. Each year, this grassroots level crowns ten regional champions and a national champion from the over one hundred short tracks that host over two thousand weekly NASCAR sanctioned races.

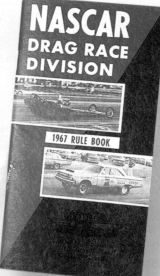

Open wheels

NASCAR's Featherlite Modified Series, middle, showcases powerful, ground-hugging racers. NASCAR has launched other series over the years. The Speedway Division gave NASCAR a home—however briefly—for Indy-cars in the 1950s, while the NASCAR Drag Racing Division was a short-lived success. Gene Darrah, above, drove a Ford Special for owner Leland Colvin.

As NASCAR rocketed toward the new millennium, it built on the successes of the past and created bold new avenues from which to access the future.

Jumping with few caution flags from one milestone to the next, stock car racing built momentum as it rode new waves of fan interest, riveting on-track competition, and dynamic drivers who were becoming household names.

Entering the closing laps of its first fifty years, NASCAR had seen its growth pattern closely follow that of the country that had such a consuming interest in automobiles and the automobile culture. Across the expanse of the United States, the post–World War II era had seen dramatic movement from a small-town society to one of booming cities, from mom-and-pop storefronts to Fortune 500 companies, from a focus on national priorities to one based on international concerns. America had grown up, flexed its muscles, seen its promise come to full flower. In professional sports, baseball, football, basketball, and hockey had been woven into the American experience, and, in its fifth decade, NASCAR took its own place at the front of the national—and international—sports stage.

As NASCAR raced into the last decade of the twentieth century, a fresh face stepped forward to take the lead. Jeff Gordon burst onto the NASCAR scene in the 1990s and became a splendid representative of what NASCAR had been, was, and could be.

MILESTONES AND MOMENTUM

Fifty plus

Embarking on its second half century, NASCAR racing pushed toward new frontiers at its 1999 NASCAR Winston Cup Series championship banquet in New York, opposite.

Gordon, whose quick rise to the top of his sport, intense driving style, and good looks created a new fan base, became one of the leaders as NASCAR enjoyed some of its most spirited seasons.

Gordon shined on the NASCAR Busch Series, Grand National Division, where he attracted enough attention to earn a rich contract offer from Hendrick Motorsports, the racing powerhouse that would launch him in NASCAR Winston Cup racing. It would become the first lifetime contract signed by a driver with a team in NASCAR Winston Cup Series history.

The Gordon story from that point to this is one of quick success, relentless achievement, and championship consistency. Schooled in the hard-knocks worlds of midget- and sprint-car racing, Gordon adapted quickly to heavier stock cars and longer races, scoring two wins for Hendrick in only his second full season (1994) of NASCAR Winston Cup racing. Those victories came in two of the season's most important events: the Coca-Cola 600 at Charlotte Motor Speedway and the inaugural Brickyard 400 at Indianapolis Motor Speedway.

That season, which showcased the powerful ties that made Gordon and his crew chief, Ray Evernham, a tremendous team, served as a prelude to 1995, when they combined for seven race wins and made Gordon—at twenty-four—the youngest NASCAR Winston Cup Series champion of the modern era. And that was only a first course for the splurge to come.

Over the next three seasons, Gordon won two more championships and a total of thirty-three races, dominating the 1998 season with thirteen victories.

There was the temptation to call Gordon an overnight success, a young invader who simply made a lucky lunge at the brass ring, but the truth is quite different. He began racing at the age of

five in California, his future mapped out by his stepfather, John Bickford. The young Gordon showed uncommon skill in quarter-midgets. By the age of thirteen, Bickford saw that the kid needed a wider field of challenge, so he moved the family to Indiana, where Gordon could race midget and sprint cars before he reached sixteen.

The Jeff Gordon story is one of quick success, relentless achievement, and championship consistency.

Gordon responded quickly. He won the United States Auto Club's midget championship in 1990 and the Silver Crown title the following season. His name and his exploits spread across the country, thanks in part to his exposure on ESPN's *Thursday Night Thunder* series. Gordon moved on to the NASCAR Busch Series, Grand National Division,

Breakthrough

Jeff Gordon (left) and team owner Rick Hendrick (right) celebrate Gordon's first NASCAR Winston Cup Series championship in 1995.

diverting from the obvious path to Indy-cars that most open-wheel short-trackers picked. In 1992, driving for future NASCAR Winston Cup team owner Bill Davis, Gordon won three NASCAR Busch Series races, writing the resume lines and showing the driving style that attracted Rick Hendrick.

From there, life became a rocket ride for Gordon. As the most visible young driver in all of motorsports, he became a magnet for sponsors and endorsements. Virtually every day of his life follows a script, dictated by race dates, practice sessions, autograph appearances, and meetings with sponsors. His life is on an accelerating platform that seldom stops.

Gordon's arrival, and his rapid success, served to illustrate the surging momentum that continued to carry NASCAR to new heights. At every turn, there seemed to be a new accomplishment, a new door to open, a new challenge to meet.

At the 1998 NASCAR Winston Cup Series awards banquet— at the end of the year in which NASCAR had celebrated its fiftieth anniversary—NASCAR president Bill France Jr. said stock car racing had reached a level on which it could rival the National Football League, the National Basketball Association, Major League Baseball, and professional golf for America's sports attention. He pointed out that the overwhelming majority of the top twenty sports events in terms of spectator attendance were NASCAR Winston Cup Series races. NASCAR attendance swelled at virtually every venue, roaring past six million (more than a threefold gain in fifteen years), while television numbers continued to show significant improvement. In the period from 1990 to 1997, for example, ratings for NASCAR events on ABC increased 62 percent.

Gordon and other new stars and key players, men like Alan Kulwicki, Mark Martin, Davey Allison, Jeff Burton, Bobby Labonte, Tony Stewart, Dale Jarrett, Jeremy Mayfield, Robert Yates, Rusty Wallace, Joe Gibbs, Jack Roush, Steve Hmiel, Robin Pemberton, Larry McReynolds, Jimmy Makar, Todd Parrott, and Ray Evernham, stepped forward to push the sport to new levels— and to new arenas, both in the United States and beyond. In the 1990s, tracks at Loudon, New Hampshire; Indianapolis, Indiana; Fort Worth, Texas; Las Vegas, Nevada; Miami, Florida; and

Other new stars and key players stepped forward to push the sport to new levels—and to new arenas.

Fontana, California, joined the NASCAR Winston Cup Series lineup, and NASCAR signed a three-year agreement to run a series of exhibition races in Japan, events that attracted a huge following on the other side of the Pacific. In the fourth year of competition in Japan, NASCAR included the overseas races in the points race for the NASCAR Winston West Series.

As the sport charged forward, NASCAR's marketing offensives, boosted by the opening of a NASCAR office in New York City, blended the spirit of tough competition with racing's broadening sponsorship representation to develop a complete entertainment experience for the expanding fan base. Racing no longer was limited to the racetrack. NASCAR SpeedPark, featuring NASCAR Winston Cup–flavored racing in go-kart-like vehicles, was launched to

Skill and experience

Team owner Robert Yates has used his engine-building skills and management ability to rack up wins with drivers like Davey Allison, Ernie Irvan, and Dale Jarrett.

give fans a taste of stock car competition from the driver's seat. Virtual racing was made available in malls across the country with NASCAR Silicon Motor Speedway, a three-quarter scale motion simulator. NASCAR Thunder stores opened in malls across the country, offering top-of-the-line clothing and other merchandise linked to America's favorite racers NASCAR Café, a themed restaurant featuring fine dining in a racing-oriented atmosphere, opened to rave reviews. NASCAR Online (www.nascar.com) debuted on the World Wide Web and immediately became the favorite stop for fans who want instant information about their favorite sport. Later, the NASCAR Online Store, an "e-commerce" store, was added to the site, giving fans access to a wide spectrum of NASCAR-licensed merchandise through the Internet. NASCAR made seven officially licensed magazines available nationwide, and popped up throughout daily television and radio listings, as a string of syndicated programs devoted to NASCAR racing responded to viewers' attraction to what was increasingly becoming known as the Sport of the 1990s. In July 1995, *Sports Illustrated*, in a cover story, labeled NASCAR Winston Cup Series racing "America's Hottest Sport."

From their cars to their cereals to their computer games, fans made the NASCAR link an ongoing part of their lives. What started on some dusty half-mile tracks far from the beaten path a half-century earlier had been transformed into a modern, mainstream American sport of the 1990s, represented by the best drivers, the best teams, and the best competition motorsports had to offer.

Just as his grandfather and father had done before him, Brian France, the third generation to carry the ball for NASCAR, stepped up to play a vital role in the sport's new chemistry.

As senior vice president, France has made the NASCAR name a familiar one in the executive suites and boardrooms of leading companies on the streets of the country's financial capital. He took the lead as NASCAR's marketing and licensing efforts exploded onto new fronts, pushing sales of officially licensed merchandise beyond the $1 billion mark. The NASCAR logo could be found on everything from books to video games to Barbie dolls to fast food, causing a revolution of sorts in the world of marketing. France shook hands and made deals with some of the leading companies in the country, putting the NASCAR name in front of the public in many new ways and forms.

In 1999, Brian France's efforts were rewarded as he was named Marketing Statesman of the Year by the Sales and Marketing Executives International organization. The award is presented each year to a corporate executive whose leadership has positively influenced the marketplace and promoted the characteristics of free enterprise.

Illustrating NASCAR's new standing was a June 1998 appearance by seven-time NASCAR Winston Cup Series champion Dale Earnhardt at a meeting of the National Press Club in Washington, D.C. Earnhardt stood at the same podium that's been graced by a long line of national and international leaders and celebrities, answering questions from some of the country's top journalists. Two years earlier, Jeff Gordon and Ray Evernham had accepted an invitation to lecture to engineering students at Princeton University, taking NASCAR to Ivy League status.

In December 1998, Bill France Jr. and several leading drivers, including Gordon and Darrell Waltrip, participated in a two-hour presentation on the history and impact of NASCAR racing at the

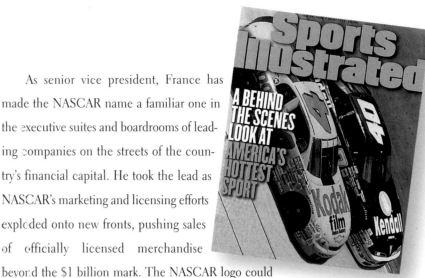

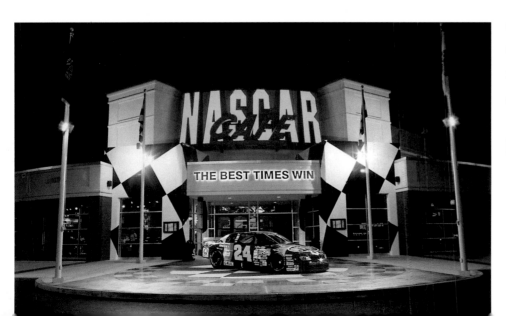

Fast food

NASCAR's soaring popularity in the 1990s led to the development of a chain of NASCAR Café restaurants, featuring fine foods and a wealth of racing memorabilia.

Smithsonian Institution. "Our trip to the Smithsonian proves that NASCAR is here to stay and ready to take its rightful position at the top of America's sports ladder," France said.

Stock car racing had reached the sort of prominence the barnstorming drivers of the 1950s saw only in their dreams.

It was, indeed, a new era. Along with the rush of large corporations eager to join the NASCAR parade as sponsors came public relations experts, marketing whizzes, and management gurus. Racing gradually became more specialized, as the sport's major teams hired experts to focus on specific areas like shock absorber development, chassis technology, and engine refinements. Team owners built massive new shop facilities, complete with plush auditoriums, fitness centers, and other amenities. Long gone were the cramped, oily one- and two-car bays that once served as team garages.

In race shops and along pit road, the ever-developing technology that had made the sport one of the safest forms of auto racing in the world continued to have an impact on week-to-week racing. Roof flaps, designed to open when a speeding car turned sideways, were developed to act as "air brakes" for cars spinning out of control. Wheel restraints were added to keep wheels from separating from cars during accidents. Tiny cameras were installed in the pits to record pit stops, enabling teams to target ways to make stops faster. Laptop computers were introduced in the pits to schedule fuel and tire stops.

This is no longer your father's Oldsmobile.

Two eras—one ending, the other beginning—crossed dramatically in the final race of the 1992 season, the Hooters 500 at Atlanta Motor Speedway on November 15, marking a watershed for NASCAR. As the sport's fan base grew into new areas, followers of the world's leading stock car racing series experienced a key changing of the guard—and much more—in one of the most extraordinary races in the history of the NASCAR Winston Cup Series.

It was the last day of driving for Richard Petty, the man who had become a legend with victory after victory in the 1960s and '70s and who now was bidding the sport farewell with a season-long "Fan Appreciation Tour." At every stop on the circuit that year, Petty, no longer winning but still flashing the ready smile that had endeared him to millions of fans, was saluted with gifts, accolades, and cascades of applause. President George Bush visited Daytona in July to see Petty's last race at one of the tracks he had mastered. He called Petty, "a king, one of the great Americans."

Now, on a fall afternoon in suburban Atlanta, Petty was driving the last mile. In an emotional drivers' meeting, he gave each of the drivers in the starting field a silver money clip inscribed with a message: "Thanks for all the memories—Richard Petty."

No one realized the full significance then, but the day also was special because another career was beginning. It was the first NASCAR Winston Cup Series race for twenty-one-year-old Jeff Gordon, who would join the tour full-time the following season.

The day turned into one of the most vivid in NASCAR Winston Cup Series history. Petty crashed less than a hundred laps into the race, a victim of others' mistakes. His car caught fire briefly, leading the King to explain that he had hoped to go out in a quite different blaze of glory. The Petty Enterprises crew repaired his battered car so he could return to the track and be rolling when the final checkered flag of his career flew. There were misty eyes all around as Petty hugged family members and, reluctantly, said good-bye to driving the No. 43 cars that he had made famous.

Gordon finished thirty-first that day at Atlanta, making no waves. His time was yet to come. Petty's was ending.

France family

NASCAR's first family is (clockwise from top) Jim France, Bill France Jr., Bill's wife, Betty Jane, son Brian, daughter Lesa, and Jim's wife Sharon. Brian France, opposite, is the third generation of the France family to take a leadership role in NASCAR.

NASCAR merchandise has gone from baseball caps and T-shirts to video games and furniture. This growth is largely the brainchild of Brian France, the third generation of the France family. Under the leadership of France, NASCAR's vice president of marketing George Pyne has heightened that growth to phenomenal levels.

From NASCAR Barbie to Coca-Cola's Racing Family six-pack, opposite, NASCAR has involved itself in complex marketing strategies that offer collectible opportunities for fans.

In 1999, NASCAR was recognized by the International Licensing Industry Merchandisers' Association (LIMA) as one of the top licensors in the industry. NASCAR was named the 1998 Sports/Special Events Licensor of the Year for the first year the association included the sports category.

The bottom line is that fans love NASCAR, and by extension, love products that represent their favorite NASCAR drivers, teams, and tracks. NASCAR has become a lifestyle away from the track for fans, and that is apparent in homes of NASCAR fans across the country. From their NASCAR recliner to their NASCAR bedspread, fans have truly welcomed America's sport into their lives.

Another Super Bowl

Dale Jarrett (left) won the 1993 Daytona 500 for car owner
Joe Gibbs (right), who had enjoyed similar successes in
leading the Washington Redskins to NFL Super Bowl victories.

Beyond the King and the Kid, there was a championship to settle. Davey Allison, Alan Kulwicki, and Bill Elliott raced into the finale with the NASCAR Winston Cup on the line. Allison's chances disappeared early with tire trouble and an accident, leaving Elliott and Kulwicki to decide it. Elliott won the race, but Kulwicki finished second and led enough laps to win the seasonal title by ten points, the smallest margin ever.

The 1993 season opened with one of the most dramatic Daytona 500s in the race's long history, as Dale Jarrett held off a charging Dale Earnhardt on the last lap to secure the victory. Adding a unique flavor to the end of the race was the presence of former driver Ned Jarrett, Dale's father, in the CBS television broadcast booth. Ned, never a winner in the 500 himself, called the final lap as his son outdueled one of racing's all-time greats to win NASCAR's biggest race: "Come on Dale. Go, baby, go. All right, come on. I know he's gone to the floorboard. He can't do any more. Come on, take her to the inside. Don't let him get on the inside of you coming around the turn. Here he comes. Earnhardt's . . . it's Dale and Dale as they come off turn four. You know who I'm pulling for as Dale Jarrett's . . . Bring her to the inside, Dale, don't let him get down there. He's going to make it . . . Dale Jarrett's going to win the Daytona 500! All right!"

The victory gave car owner Joe Gibbs, who also was coach of NFL's Washington Redskins, a unique double: Daytona 500 and Super Bowl championships.

> "He's going to make it . . . Dale Jarrett's going to win the Daytona 500! All right!"
>
> — RACING ANNOUNCER AND FATHER NED JARRETT

Although a big day for the Jarrett clan, the 1993 500 was another in a long line of disappointments for Dale Earnhardt in the Super Bowl of stock car racing. Despite winning dozens of other races at Daytona, Earnhardt mysteriously had failed to score in the 500 for two decades, losing the victory several times in bizarre circumstances. No loss was more painful than the one he endured in the 1990 race, when an exploding tire in the third turn of the final lap dropped him from the lead, opening the door to an unlikely victory by Derrike Cope, who, before that Sunday, had had no top-five finishes.

Against a backdrop of astonishing successes and momentum, there were some hard rains to endure. The 1993 season saw the painful losses of two of the sport's most accomplished young drivers. Alan Kulwicki, who had surprised racing by pushing his own team to the 1992 NASCAR Winston Cup Series championship, died April 1 in the crash of a private plane en route to a race in Bristol, Tennessee. Davey Allison, a winner nineteen times in NASCAR Winston Cup racing, sustained serious injuries in a helicopter crash that summer in Talladega, Alabama, and died the following day.

The unusual racing journey of driver Ernie Irvan covered much of the 1990s. After establishing himself as one of the top drivers on the tour early in the decade, Irvan saw his progress stopped on August 20, 1994, when he was injured in an accident at Michigan Speedway. After a remarkable fourteen-month recovery—few thought there was any hope he would ever race again—Irvan returned to NASCAR Winston Cup Series racing as a driver. At New Hampshire in 1996, he won again, then visited victory lane at Michigan in 1997, chasing the last demons of his accident. Two years later, Irvan retired, two more wrecks having signaled to him that the right decision was the one to quit.

Comeback kid

Ernie Irvan, left, with wife Kim, provided one of the most inspirational stories of the 1990s, recovering from injuries in a 1994 crash to race again—and win again—later in the decade. He retired in 1999.

Leading NASCAR Winston Cup Series teams put hundreds of thousands of dollars into the building of supertough engines every year, top and opposite. In the final analysis, secrets learned in the engine-building process often make the difference between winning and losing.

A winning car's journey to victory lane begins many months before, within the walls of some of the most elaborate motorsports shops in the world. Members of Richard Childress's Racing team weld parts of the frame of Dale Earnhardt's No. 3 Chevrolets, middle, and put sheet metal pieces on one of Dale Earnhardt's No. 3 Chevrolets, bottom.

To the Brickyard

NASCAR rolled onto the revered asphalt (and bricks) of Indianapolis Motor Speedway in 1994, beginning a successful marriage between one of the world's most famous motorsports showplaces and America's favorite form of racing.

Critical to NASCAR's soaring growth pattern in the 1990s was expansion to new areas of the country, and nowhere was that effort more important than in stock car racing's invasion of Indianapolis Motor Speedway (IMS), for almost a century an exclusive haven for open-wheel racers. NASCAR's first race at the historic track was one of stock car racing's grandest moments.

Flirtation between the two racing giants, NASCAR and Indy, had been ongoing for several years before nine NASCAR Winston Cup teams gathered at the hallowed Brickyard in June 1992 to run what was officially billed as a Goodyear tire test. The two days at IMS would determine whether or not the 2.5-mile rectangular track and the big stock cars were suitable matches for each other. The test sessions went well—more than fifty thousand fans showed up at the track just to see practice laps—and it seemed inevitable that a NASCAR Winston Cup Series race would be scheduled at the track.

The first Brickyard 400 was announced in grand fashion by track president Tony George and NASCAR president Bill France

> **Flirtation between racing giants NASCAR and Indy had been ongoing for years when NASCAR teams gathered at the hallowed Brickyard.**

Jr. It was scheduled for August 6, 1994. Hundreds of thousands of available tickets were gobbled up within hours.

The biggest crowd in NASCAR history—more than three hundred thousand fans—jammed into the sprawling IMS facility that August day to see the meeting of two great traditions: Indy's storied racetrack and NASCAR's tight stock car competition. Addressing the drivers' meeting before the race, France told the competitors in attendance that "everyone in the world will be watching us here. . . . You guys are a part of history. You're carrying the name for NASCAR. I'm proud to know you, and I'm proud to be a part of you."

The race was a bell-ringer. The win went to Jeff Gordon, who had lived down the road in Pittsboro, Indiana, during his teenage racing years. Gordon described himself as "a kid in a candy store," standing in a victory lane he had dreamed of visiting as a child. As Gordon made his final lap, the cheering from the hundreds of thousands in the sprawling grandstands could be heard above the sound of his engine.

The 1994 season saw Dale Earnhardt claim his seventh NASCAR Winston Cup Series championship, tying Richard Petty in the category of most titles won. Earnhardt won four races and finished in the top five twenty times, the sort of consistency the NASCAR Winston Cup Series point system rewards.

The 1994 season had its valleys as the sport lost drivers Neil Bonnett and Rodney Orr. And popular driver Harry Gant, who started NASCAR Winston Cup Series racing relatively late in his career but accumulated eighteen victories and a large fan base, retired at the end of the season.

Handsome Harry

North Carolina driver Harry Gant became one of the most popular drivers in the early 1990s after he garnered a string of wins in four consecutive races.

The Brickyard

With grandstands filled to capacity and its huge scoring tower reaching for the sky, Indianapolis Motor Speedway hears the roar of stock car thunder.

In the mid-1990s, NASCAR Winston Cup Series racing was transformed by the phenomenon of multicar teams, a development that propelled the sport in a new direction. It wasn't an original idea—team owners had raced more than one car as far back as the 1950s—but the execution was new and bold. For most of two decades, drivers generally had criticized the concept of multicar teams, saying a team didn't stand a chance of winning unless every person on the team was committed to the success of a single driver. That point of view changed rapidly in the 1990s, as team after team proved the theory that more is better. Rick Hendrick, Jack Roush, and Robert Yates made the concept work, and others followed. By the end of the decade, the multicar idea was such a success that single-car teams were considered near relics.

Terry Labonte drove one of those multicar operations, Hendrick Motorsports, to the NASCAR Winston Cup Series championship in 1996, notching his second national title and reaching another remarkable landmark along the way. In April, Labonte broke Richard Petty's record of starting 513 consecutive NASCAR Winston Cup races, and, as the millennium approached, he showed no signs of slowing down. With Jeff Gordon winning the championship in 1995, '97, and '98, Hendrick could boast of four consecutive title seasons. In 1998, Gordon won thirteen times, becoming the only driver in the modern era to win ten or more races in three consecutive seasons. Gordon's thirteen victories tied Richard Petty's modern era record.

> By the end of the decade, the multicar idea was such a success that single-car teams were considered near-relics.

As NASCAR moved forward, a part of its heralded past was left behind as North Wilkesboro Speedway in the Brushy Mountains of North Carolina hosted its final NASCAR Winston Cup Series race on September 29, 1996. The track, one of NASCAR's originals, had been purchased by Bruton Smith and Bob Bahre, and its two NASCAR Winston Cup Series dates were switched to Texas Motor Speedway, operated by Smith, and New Hampshire International Speedway, Bahre's track. North Wilkesboro faded into the moonlight of the southern Appalachians, its twin histories of racing and moonshine at an end.

In 1998, NASCAR staged a yearlong celebration of its first half-century, an observance highlighted by the selection of the top fifty drivers of the first fifty years. Dale Earnhardt was one of the fabulous fifty, and he kicked off the anniversary year in stirring fashion, finally winning the event that had eluded him for two decades: the Daytona 500.

Circumstances most foul had bitten Earnhardt in previous 500s, and there were those who were predicting that his excellent career might end without a win in his sport's most important race. But Earnhardt was ready when his moment came. He outran Bobby Labonte to the yellow flag as the 1998 race ended under caution, starting a celebration that would last for days. As Earnhardt rolled down pit road on his way to victory lane, crewmen from virtually every team swarmed his car, reaching for the chance to congratulate one of racing's greatest heroes at perhaps his greatest moment and illustrating the climate of true family sportsmanship the sport has always fostered.

In a NASCAR driver questionnaire he completed prior to the 1975 season, his first in NASCAR Winston Cup Series

A racing capital

Hendrick Motorsports, located in a massive complex near Charlotte, North Carolina, left, started a trend in the 1990s by proving that multicar teams could succeed. Bright red and yellow Chevrolets prepared for Terry Labonte wait in the No. 5 shop, opposite.

racing, Earnhardt had written "None" beside the line asking him to describe his "ambition other than racing." In the twilight of that Daytona afternoon almost a quarter-century later, he had realized one of his fondest dreams.

The fiftieth anniversary celebration, started with such perfection by Earnhardt, rolled on. It included numerous special events, highlighted by "NASCAR's Night in Hollywood," a star-spangled celebration that included television and film personalities Martin Sheen, Craig T. Nelson, Tim Allen, Don Johnson, James Woods, and numerous other performers. During the program, NASCAR honored its "drivers of the decade" for the first fifty years, a celebration that was the first of its kind for any professional sport. Herb Thomas (1950s), Richard Petty (1960s), Cale Yarborough (1970s), Darrell Waltrip (1980s), and Dale Earnhardt (1990s) were featured in the two-hour, primetime event televised by ESPN.

The 1998 season also marked a dramatic change at Daytona International Speedway, for almost forty years the sport's landmark track. Speedway officials decided to add a lighting system to the 2.5-mile facility for the 1998 Pepsi 400, a decision that startled many but turned out to be a major hit. Racing at night allowed fans to avoid the oppressive midday heat that had plagued other summer races at Daytona, and drivers were pleased with the cooler temperatures and the added thrill of driving under the lights at one of auto racing's fastest speedways. Although raging wildfires in central Florida forced postponement of the first 400 run under the lights from July until October, the event was a big success, drawing a sellout crowd and showcasing dynamic nighttime racing.

The 1999 season opened with a flurry of excitement, largely because there was another Earnhardt in town. Dale Earnhardt Jr., son of the seven-time NASCAR Winston Cup Series champion, made his NASCAR Winston Cup Series debut in May at Charlotte after enjoying championship success in the NASCAR Busch

Series, Grand National Division. The younger Earnhardt's arrival produced unprecedented media coverage. Never in the history of the sport had a driver's first race been talked about and written about in so many places.

It was another milestone. And more momentum.

The future of NASCAR will be written by drivers like Dale Earnhardt Jr., Matt Kenseth, Tony Stewart, and Adam Petty, the fourth generation of his family to race a stock car and now a crafty "veteran" at nineteen years old. Adam sat for an interview at the age of twelve, when he was getting a taste for motorsports by racing go-karts. Not yet a teenager, Adam already showed the Petty pizzazz for cutting to the heart of the deal. "This guy I was talking to runs a go-kart company," he explained. "He said if I put a sticker on my cart and on my uniform and on my trailer, he'll give me a new cart for two hundred bucks." His mother, Patti, jumped

Finally, the big one

After two decades of disappointment, Dale Earnhardt won the biggest race of all, the Daytona 500, in 1998. Rival crewmen greeted Earnhardt on pit road, above, before he and car owner Richard Childress, opposite, began a joyous celebration in victory lane.

Across the Pacific

NASCAR heightened its international presence by scheduling a series of exhibition races in Japan in 1996, '97, and '98. The trips across the Pacific proved the emerging strength of driver Mike Skinner (No. 31), who won two of the races, underlined the fact that there are Earnhardt fans everywhere, and showed that NASCAR's brand of stock car racing will play to a variety of audiences. In 1999, the Winston West Series held its first points race in Japan.

in to explain the ins and outs of a twelve-year-old racing go-karts and how the family had determined that he should be just a regular kid for a while longer, before the racing bug bit full-time. "It's my interview, Mom," insisted Adam.

The young Petty's time would come seven years later, when he raced a full-time NASCAR Busch Series, Grand National Division schedule, the next in a formidable line of Pettys to ride the NASCAR wave.

NASCAR took a big step toward the future February 10, 1999, with the naming of Mike Helton to the position of senior vice president and chief operating officer of NASCAR. Helton is a familiar figure in NASCAR Winston Cup Series garages, having been NASCAR's vice president for competition and, before that, serving in numerous positions at NASCAR Winston Cup speedways. But his promotion to chief operating officer was a landmark moment: It marked the first time in NASCAR's fifty-one-year history that day-to-day operations of the sanctioning body had been under the control of someone other than a France family member. Bill France Jr. remained as NASCAR president, but Helton inherited much of the organization's decision-making authority. He arrived in the job with a busy racing background—stints in public relations at Atlanta Motor Speedway, in marketing at Daytona International Speedway, as the general manager of Talladega Superspeedway, and as vice president for competition for all NASCAR divisions.

> It marked the first time that day-to-day operations of NASCAR were under the control of someone other than a France family member.

Helton took charge at a time of unparalleled growth, with important decisions to be made about NASCAR's future in relation to television, the length and breadth of its NASCAR Winston Cup Series schedule, and the posture it will take as the new millennium arrives.

"You try to look five years down the road, and it's not easy to do for several reasons," Helton said. "With the amount of growth that has occurred, it's hard to sit here and try to manage the elements that have gotten us to this moment. There are so many of them. Things have gone so well that it's hard to look five years down the road and say this is what we want to be doing.

"Obviously, we want to keep growing NASCAR. By growing it, you try to be very careful in the market areas that NASCAR will participate in with races and with the facilities that it's doing business with today. How do you keep those facilities growing so that you not only grow new business but you grow with the business you already have, too?"

New man at the top

Mike Helton, left with Bill France Jr., was named NASCAR chief operating officer in February 1999 and will oversee NASCAR's ride into the twenty-first century.

Running toward the future

Tony Stewart moved into NASCAR from open-wheel racing and stunned observers by winning three events in his rookie season in 1999.

With numerous speedways and proposed speedways trying to line up for NASCAR Winston Cup Series dates and other tracks hoping to add one, decisions about the future shape of the schedule will be critical. NASCAR wants to race near New York City, Chicago, Kansas City, Denver, and possibly other major market areas but must deal with the limitations presented by the calendar and the clock. There are only so many raceable weekends in a year, and teams have only so many hours to build, refine, and transport race cars to race sites.

"We'll grow it one or two steps at a time until we feel like, 'That's it,'" Helton said. "One day we'll have more races and we'll walk through the garage area and talk to different people and players and we'll know that we've gone as far as we can go. But we're not there right now."

Helton has seen the NASCAR experience change dramatically over the past decade, with new drivers, new teams, new speedways, and new approaches sparking broader interest in the sport that began a half-century ago on Carolina dirt tracks and Daytona Beach sand. The future offers even more promise, but, said Helton, NASCAR's strength will be based on a solid foundation.

"Like any other strong business, we have continuity," he said. "For forty-something years, we've raced at Darlington. For forty-something years, we've raced at Daytona. We've got continuity with the facilities, and we've got continuity with the guys that sell the tickets. That's a Richard Petty and a Cale Yarborough and a David Pearson and a Dale Earnhardt and a Darrell Waltrip and a Bill Elliott and a Rusty Wallace. Then we see Jeff Gordon and Jeff Burton and Bobby Labonte getting better every day, and we see talents like Tony Stewart coming along every day."

NASCAR has stretched the wings of Bill France's dream to become a vibrant, growing force in the American sports scene.

As the turn of the century beckons, NASCAR is poised for even greater growth. It is housed in a massive headquarters building across the street from Daytona International Speedway. It's NASCAR's fourth office location in Daytona, and it's a far cry from the home-based headquarters Bill France Sr. and Anne B., his wife, opened a half-century ago as stock car racing was making its infant steps toward an unknown future.

At the reception desk at the NASCAR headquarters entrance, visitors can pick up information sheets about the nearby Daytona USA tourist attraction. The papers are printed in English, Spanish, German, and Japanese—a small but telling sign of how far NASCAR has come. And how far it yet can go.

Big Bill France could never have imagined that the organization he first dreamed about—a sanctioning body that would make racing more business-like and efficient—would one day become the empire that is the modern NASCAR. France likely would marvel at the vast range of opportunities now available for talented young racers who dream much the same dream he had—of stock car racing as a viable, powerful, American sport, built from the hard work and hard driving of adventurous competitors.

From the dirt tracks to Daytona and from the sands of the Atlantic shore to New York's financial district, NASCAR has stretched the wings of Bill France's dream to become a vibrant, growing force on the American sports scene. The road to the future, leading to the challenges and opportunities of a new millennium, holds only green flags.

Sparkle and pop

Jeff Gordon won the 1998 Pepsi 400 under the lights at
Daytona, opposite and following spread, igniting a vivid
primetime celebration in victory lane and dramatically
illustrating how far NASCAR had come in its first fifty years.

PHOTOGRAPHY CREDITS